THIS IS YOUR **PASSBOOK®** FOR ...

HABILITATION SPECIALIST

NATIONAL LEARNING CORPORATION®
passbooks.com

PASSBOOK® SERIES

THE *PASSBOOK® SERIES* has been created to prepare applicants and candidates for the ultimate academic battlefield – the examination room.

At some time in our lives, each and every one of us may be required to take an examination – for validation, matriculation, admission, qualification, registration, certification, or licensure.

Based on the assumption that every applicant or candidate has met the basic formal educational standards, has taken the required number of courses, and read the necessary texts, the *PASSBOOK® SERIES* furnishes the one special preparation which may assure passing with confidence, instead of failing with insecurity. Examination questions – together with answers – are furnished as the basic vehicle for study so that the mysteries of the examination and its compounding difficulties may be eliminated or diminished by a sure method.

This book is meant to help you pass your examination provided that you qualify and are serious in your objective.

The entire field is reviewed through the huge store of content information which is succinctly presented through a provocative and challenging approach – the question-and-answer method.

A climate of success is established by furnishing the correct answers at the end of each test.

You soon learn to recognize types of questions, forms of questions, and patterns of questioning. You may even begin to anticipate expected outcomes.

You perceive that many questions are repeated or adapted so that you can gain acute insights, which may enable you to score many sure points.

You learn how to confront new questions, or types of questions, and to attack them confidently and work out the correct answers.

You note objectives and emphases, and recognize pitfalls and dangers, so that you may make positive educational adjustments.

Moreover, you are kept fully informed in relation to new concepts, methods, practices, and directions in the field.

You discover that you arre actually taking the examination all the time: you are preparing for the examination by "taking" an examination, not by reading extraneous and/or supererogatory textbooks.

In short, this PASSBOOK®, used directedly, should be an important factor in helping you to pass your test.

HABILITATION SPECIALIST

DUTIES:

As a Habilitation Specialist, you would work with individuals with developmental disabilities to help them lead better lives. You would instruct and guide these individuals in developing basic learning and self-help skills, as well as communication, community, and prevocational skills. In addition, you would help individuals reach their optimal level of functioning by assisting in goal setting after a functional assessment, assisting in the development and evaluation of habilitation plans consistent with Individual Service Plans (ISPs), and monitoring and recording individual progress. You may also instruct and observe direct care staff in employing appropriate strategies with individuals consistent with their habilitation plans.

SCOPE OF THE EXAMINATION:

The written test is designed to test for knowledge, skills, and/or abilities in such areas as:

1. **Developing and implementing habilitation plans** - These questions test for the ability to develop, implement, and evaluate habilitation plans that address the needs of people with developmental disabilities. Questions may cover such topics as assessing needs and strengths, using this assessment to develop individualized habilitation goals and plans, selecting and applying appropriate training methods and behavior modification techniques, helping people achieve their goals, and overseeing direct care.
2. **Understanding and interpreting written material** - These questions test how well you comprehend written material. You will be provided with brief reading selections and will be asked questions about the selections. All the information required to answer the questions will be presented in the selections; you will not be required to have any special knowledge relating to the subject areas of the selections.
3. **Coding information** - These questions test for the ability to use written directions to code information accurately. You will be asked to apply one or more sets of coding rules. Complete directions are provided; no previous knowledge of, or training in, any coding system is required.

HOW TO TAKE A TEST

I. YOU MUST PASS AN EXAMINATION

A. WHAT EVERY CANDIDATE SHOULD KNOW

Examination applicants often ask us for help in preparing for the written test. What can I study in advance? What kinds of questions will be asked? How will the test be given? How will the papers be graded?

As an applicant for a civil service examination, you may be wondering about some of these things. Our purpose here is to suggest effective methods of advance study and to describe civil service examinations.

Your chances for success on this examination can be increased if you know how to prepare. Those "pre-examination jitters" can be reduced if you know what to expect. You can even experience an adventure in good citizenship if you know why civil service exams are given.

B. WHY ARE CIVIL SERVICE EXAMINATIONS GIVEN?

Civil service examinations are important to you in two ways. As a citizen, you want public jobs filled by employees who know how to do their work. As a job seeker, you want a fair chance to compete for that job on an equal footing with other candidates. The best-known means of accomplishing this two-fold goal is the competitive examination.

Exams are widely publicized throughout the nation. They may be administered for jobs in federal, state, city, municipal, town or village governments or agencies.

Any citizen may apply, with some limitations, such as the age or residence of applicants. Your experience and education may be reviewed to see whether you meet the requirements for the particular examination. When these requirements exist, they are reasonable and applied consistently to all applicants. Thus, a competitive examination may cause you some uneasiness now, but it is your privilege and safeguard.

C. HOW ARE CIVIL SERVICE EXAMS DEVELOPED?

Examinations are carefully written by trained technicians who are specialists in the field known as "psychological measurement," in consultation with recognized authorities in the field of work that the test will cover. These experts recommend the subject matter areas or skills to be tested; only those knowledges or skills important to your success on the job are included. The most reliable books and source materials available are used as references. Together, the experts and technicians judge the difficulty level of the questions.

Test technicians know how to phrase questions so that the problem is clearly stated. Their ethics do not permit "trick" or "catch" questions. Questions may have been tried out on sample groups, or subjected to statistical analysis, to determine their usefulness.

Written tests are often used in combination with performance tests, ratings of training and experience, and oral interviews. All of these measures combine to form the best-known means of finding the right person for the right job.

II. HOW TO PASS THE WRITTEN TEST

A. NATURE OF THE EXAMINATION

To prepare intelligently for civil service examinations, you should know how they differ from school examinations you have taken. In school you were assigned certain definite pages to read or subjects to cover. The examination questions were quite detailed and usually emphasized memory. Civil service exams, on the other hand, try to discover your present ability to perform the duties of a position, plus your potentiality to learn these duties. In other words, a civil service exam attempts to predict how successful you will be. Questions cover such a broad area that they cannot be as minute and detailed as school exam questions.

In the public service similar kinds of work, or positions, are grouped together in one "class." This process is known as *position-classification*. All the positions in a class are paid according to the salary range for that class. One class title covers all of these positions, and they are all tested by the same examination.

B. FOUR BASIC STEPS

1) Study the announcement

How, then, can you know what subjects to study? Our best answer is: "Learn as much as possible about the class of positions for which you've applied." The exam will test the knowledge, skills and abilities needed to do the work.

Your most valuable source of information about the position you want is the official exam announcement. This announcement lists the training and experience qualifications. Check these standards and apply only if you come reasonably close to meeting them.

The brief description of the position in the examination announcement offers some clues to the subjects which will be tested. Think about the job itself. Review the duties in your mind. Can you perform them, or are there some in which you are rusty? Fill in the blank spots in your preparation.

Many jurisdictions preview the written test in the exam announcement by including a section called "Knowledge and Abilities Required," "Scope of the Examination," or some similar heading. Here you will find out specifically what fields will be tested.

2) Review your own background

Once you learn in general what the position is all about, and what you need to know to do the work, ask yourself which subjects you already know fairly well and which need improvement. You may wonder whether to concentrate on improving your strong areas or on building some background in your fields of weakness. When the announcement has specified "some knowledge" or "considerable knowledge," or has used adjectives like "beginning principles of…" or "advanced … methods," you can get a clue as to the number and difficulty of questions to be asked in any given field. More questions, and hence broader coverage, would be included for those subjects which are more important in the work. Now weigh your strengths and weaknesses against the job requirements and prepare accordingly.

3) Determine the level of the position

Another way to tell how intensively you should prepare is to understand the level of the job for which you are applying. Is it the entering level? In other words, is this the position in which beginners in a field of work are hired? Or is it an intermediate or advanced level? Sometimes this is indicated by such words as "Junior" or "Senior" in the class title. Other jurisdictions use Roman numerals to designate the level – Clerk I, Clerk II, for example. The word "Supervisor" sometimes appears in the title. If the level is not indicated by the title, check the description of duties. Will you be working under very close supervision, or will you have responsibility for independent decisions in this work?

4) Choose appropriate study materials

Now that you know the subjects to be examined and the relative amount of each subject to be covered, you can choose suitable study materials. For beginning level jobs, or even advanced ones, if you have a pronounced weakness in some aspect of your training, read a modern, standard textbook in that field. Be sure it is up to date and has general coverage. Such books are normally available at your library, and the librarian will be glad to help you locate one. For entry-level positions, questions of appropriate difficulty are chosen – neither highly advanced questions, nor those too simple. Such questions require careful thought but not advanced training.

If the position for which you are applying is technical or advanced, you will read more advanced, specialized material. If you are already familiar with the basic principles of your field, elementary textbooks would waste your time. Concentrate on advanced textbooks and technical periodicals. Think through the concepts and review difficult problems in your field.

These are all general sources. You can get more ideas on your own initiative, following these leads. For example, training manuals and publications of the government agency which employs workers in your field can be useful, particularly for technical and professional positions. A letter or visit to the government department involved may result in more specific study suggestions, and certainly will provide you with a more definite idea of the exact nature of the position you are seeking.

III. KINDS OF TESTS

Tests are used for purposes other than measuring knowledge and ability to perform specified duties. For some positions, it is equally important to test ability to make adjustments to new situations or to profit from training. In others, basic mental abilities not dependent on information are essential. Questions which test these things may not appear as pertinent to the duties of the position as those which test for knowledge and information. Yet they are often highly important parts of a fair examination. For very general questions, it is almost impossible to help you direct your study efforts. What we can do is to point out some of the more common of these general abilities needed in public service positions and describe some typical questions.

1) General information

Broad, general information has been found useful for predicting job success in some kinds of work. This is tested in a variety of ways, from vocabulary lists to questions about current events. Basic background in some field of work, such as sociology or economics, may be sampled in a group of questions. Often these are principles which have become familiar to most persons through exposure rather than through formal training. It is difficult to advise you how to study for these questions; being alert to the world around you is our best suggestion.

2) Verbal ability

An example of an ability needed in many positions is verbal or language ability. Verbal ability is, in brief, the ability to use and understand words. Vocabulary and grammar tests are typical measures of this ability. Reading comprehension or paragraph interpretation questions are common in many kinds of civil service tests. You are given a paragraph of written material and asked to find its central meaning.

3) Numerical ability

Number skills can be tested by the familiar arithmetic problem, by checking paired lists of numbers to see which are alike and which are different, or by interpreting charts and graphs. In the latter test, a graph may be printed in the test booklet which you are asked to use as the basis for answering questions.

4) Observation

A popular test for law-enforcement positions is the observation test. A picture is shown to you for several minutes, then taken away. Questions about the picture test your ability to observe both details and larger elements.

5) Following directions

In many positions in the public service, the employee must be able to carry out written instructions dependably and accurately. You may be given a chart with several columns, each column listing a variety of information. The questions require you to carry out directions involving the information given in the chart.

6) Skills and aptitudes

Performance tests effectively measure some manual skills and aptitudes. When the skill is one in which you are trained, such as typing or shorthand, you can practice. These tests are often very much like those given in business school or high school courses. For many of the other skills and aptitudes, however, no short-time preparation can be made. Skills and abilities natural to you or that you have developed throughout your lifetime are being tested.

Many of the general questions just described provide all the data needed to answer the questions and ask you to use your reasoning ability to find the answers. Your best preparation for these tests, as well as for tests of facts and ideas, is to be at your physical and mental best. You, no doubt, have your own methods of getting into an exam-taking mood and keeping "in shape." The next section lists some ideas on this subject.

IV. KINDS OF QUESTIONS

Only rarely is the "essay" question, which you answer in narrative form, used in civil service tests. Civil service tests are usually of the short-answer type. Full instructions for answering these questions will be given to you at the examination. But in case this is your first experience with short-answer questions and separate answer sheets, here is what you need to know:

1) Multiple-choice Questions

Most popular of the short-answer questions is the "multiple choice" or "best answer" question. It can be used, for example, to test for factual knowledge, ability to solve problems or judgment in meeting situations found at work.

A multiple-choice question is normally one of three types—

- It can begin with an incomplete statement followed by several possible endings. You are to find the one ending which *best* completes the statement, although some of the others may not be entirely wrong.
- It can also be a complete statement in the form of a question which is answered by choosing one of the statements listed.
- It can be in the form of a problem – again you select the best answer.

Here is an example of a multiple-choice question with a discussion which should give you some clues as to the method for choosing the right answer:

When an employee has a complaint about his assignment, the action which will *best* help him overcome his difficulty is to
- A. discuss his difficulty with his coworkers
- B. take the problem to the head of the organization
- C. take the problem to the person who gave him the assignment
- D. say nothing to anyone about his complaint

In answering this question, you should study each of the choices to find which is best. Consider choice "A" – Certainly an employee may discuss his complaint with fellow employees, but no change or improvement can result, and the complaint remains unresolved. Choice "B" is a poor choice since the head of the organization probably does not know what assignment you have been given, and taking your problem to him is known as "going over the head" of the supervisor. The supervisor, or person who made the assignment, is the person who can clarify it or correct any injustice. Choice "C" is, therefore, correct. To say nothing, as in choice "D," is unwise. Supervisors have and interest in knowing the problems employees are facing, and the employee is seeking a solution to his problem.

2) True/False Questions

The "true/false" or "right/wrong" form of question is sometimes used. Here a complete statement is given. Your job is to decide whether the statement is right or wrong.

SAMPLE: A roaming cell-phone call to a nearby city costs less than a non-roaming call to a distant city.

This statement is wrong, or false, since roaming calls are more expensive.
This is not a complete list of all possible question forms, although most of the others are variations of these common types. You will always get complete directions for

answering questions. Be sure you understand *how* to mark your answers – ask questions until you do.

V. RECORDING YOUR ANSWERS

Computer terminals are used more and more today for many different kinds of exams.

For an examination with very few applicants, you may be told to record your answers in the test booklet itself. Separate answer sheets are much more common. If this separate answer sheet is to be scored by machine – and this is often the case – it is highly important that you mark your answers correctly in order to get credit.

An electronic scoring machine is often used in civil service offices because of the speed with which papers can be scored. Machine-scored answer sheets must be marked with a pencil, which will be given to you. This pencil has a high graphite content which responds to the electronic scoring machine. As a matter of fact, stray dots may register as answers, so do not let your pencil rest on the answer sheet while you are pondering the correct answer. Also, if your pencil lead breaks or is otherwise defective, ask for another.

Since the answer sheet will be dropped in a slot in the scoring machine, be careful not to bend the corners or get the paper crumpled.

The answer sheet normally has five vertical columns of numbers, with 30 numbers to a column. These numbers correspond to the question numbers in your test booklet. After each number, going across the page are four or five pairs of dotted lines. These short dotted lines have small letters or numbers above them. The first two pairs may also have a "T" or "F" above the letters. This indicates that the first two pairs only are to be used if the questions are of the true-false type. If the questions are multiple choice, disregard the "T" and "F" and pay attention only to the small letters or numbers.

Answer your questions in the manner of the sample that follows:

32. The largest city in the United States is
    A. Washington, D.C.
    B. New York City
    C. Chicago
    D. Detroit
    E. San Francisco

1) Choose the answer you think is best. (New York City is the largest, so "B" is correct.)
2) Find the row of dotted lines numbered the same as the question you are answering. (Find row number 32)
3) Find the pair of dotted lines corresponding to the answer. (Find the pair of lines under the mark "B.")
4) Make a solid black mark between the dotted lines.

VI. BEFORE THE TEST

Common sense will help you find procedures to follow to get ready for an examination. Too many of us, however, overlook these sensible measures. Indeed, nervousness and fatigue have been found to be the most serious reasons why applicants fail to do their best on civil service tests. Here is a list of reminders:

- Begin your preparation early – Don't wait until the last minute to go scurrying around for books and materials or to find out what the position is all about.
- Prepare continuously – An hour a night for a week is better than an all-night cram session. This has been definitely established. What is more, a night a week for a month will return better dividends than crowding your study into a shorter period of time.
- Locate the place of the exam – You have been sent a notice telling you when and where to report for the examination. If the location is in a different town or otherwise unfamiliar to you, it would be well to inquire the best route and learn something about the building.
- Relax the night before the test – Allow your mind to rest. Do not study at all that night. Plan some mild recreation or diversion; then go to bed early and get a good night's sleep.
- Get up early enough to make a leisurely trip to the place for the test – This way unforeseen events, traffic snarls, unfamiliar buildings, etc. will not upset you.
- Dress comfortably – A written test is not a fashion show. You will be known by number and not by name, so wear something comfortable.
- Leave excess paraphernalia at home – Shopping bags and odd bundles will get in your way. You need bring only the items mentioned in the official notice you received; usually everything you need is provided. Do not bring reference books to the exam. They will only confuse those last minutes and be taken away from you when in the test room.
- Arrive somewhat ahead of time – If because of transportation schedules you must get there very early, bring a newspaper or magazine to take your mind off yourself while waiting.
- Locate the examination room – When you have found the proper room, you will be directed to the seat or part of the room where you will sit. Sometimes you are given a sheet of instructions to read while you are waiting. Do not fill out any forms until you are told to do so; just read them and be prepared.
- Relax and prepare to listen to the instructions
- If you have any physical problem that may keep you from doing your best, be sure to tell the test administrator. If you are sick or in poor health, you really cannot do your best on the exam. You can come back and take the test some other time.

VII. AT THE TEST

The day of the test is here and you have the test booklet in your hand. The temptation to get going is very strong. Caution! There is more to success than knowing the right answers. You must know how to identify your papers and understand variations in the type of short-answer question used in this particular examination. Follow these suggestions for maximum results from your efforts:

1) Cooperate with the monitor

The test administrator has a duty to create a situation in which you can be as much at ease as possible. He will give instructions, tell you when to begin, check to see that you are marking your answer sheet correctly, and so on. He is not there to guard you, although he will see that your competitors do not take unfair advantage. He wants to help you do your best.

2) Listen to all instructions

Don't jump the gun! Wait until you understand all directions. In most civil service tests you get more time than you need to answer the questions. So don't be in a hurry. Read each word of instructions until you clearly understand the meaning. Study the examples, listen to all announcements and follow directions. Ask questions if you do not understand what to do.

3) Identify your papers

Civil service exams are usually identified by number only. You will be assigned a number; you must not put your name on your test papers. Be sure to copy your number correctly. Since more than one exam may be given, copy your exact examination title.

4) Plan your time

Unless you are told that a test is a "speed" or "rate of work" test, speed itself is usually not important. Time enough to answer all the questions will be provided, but this does not mean that you have all day. An overall time limit has been set. Divide the total time (in minutes) by the number of questions to determine the approximate time you have for each question.

5) Do not linger over difficult questions

If you come across a difficult question, mark it with a paper clip (useful to have along) and come back to it when you have been through the booklet. One caution if you do this – be sure to skip a number on your answer sheet as well. Check often to be sure that you have not lost your place and that you are marking in the row numbered the same as the question you are answering.

6) Read the questions

Be sure you know what the question asks! Many capable people are unsuccessful because they failed to *read* the questions correctly.

7) Answer all questions

Unless you have been instructed that a penalty will be deducted for incorrect answers, it is better to guess than to omit a question.

8) Speed tests

It is often better NOT to guess on speed tests. It has been found that on timed tests people are tempted to spend the last few seconds before time is called in marking answers at random – without even reading them – in the hope of picking up a few extra points. To discourage this practice, the instructions may warn you that your score will be "corrected" for guessing. That is, a penalty will be applied. The incorrect answers will be deducted from the correct ones, or some other penalty formula will be used.

9) Review your answers

If you finish before time is called, go back to the questions you guessed or omitted to give them further thought. Review other answers if you have time.

10) Return your test materials

If you are ready to leave before others have finished or time is called, take ALL your materials to the monitor and leave quietly. Never take any test material with you. The monitor can discover whose papers are not complete, and taking a test booklet may be grounds for disqualification.

VIII. EXAMINATION TECHNIQUES

1) Read the general instructions carefully. These are usually printed on the first page of the exam booklet. As a rule, these instructions refer to the timing of the examination; the fact that you should not start work until the signal and must stop work at a signal, etc. If there are any *special* instructions, such as a choice of questions to be answered, make sure that you note this instruction carefully.

2) When you are ready to start work on the examination, that is as soon as the signal has been given, read the instructions to each question booklet, underline any key words or phrases, such as *least, best, outline, describe* and the like. In this way you will tend to answer as requested rather than discover on reviewing your paper that you *listed without describing*, that you selected the *worst* choice rather than the *best* choice, etc.

3) If the examination is of the objective or multiple-choice type – that is, each question will also give a series of possible answers: A, B, C or D, and you are called upon to select the best answer and write the letter next to that answer on your answer paper – it is advisable to start answering each question in turn. There may be anywhere from 50 to 100 such questions in the three or four hours allotted and you can see how much time would be taken if you read through all the questions before beginning to answer any. Furthermore, if you come across a question or group of questions which you know would be difficult to answer, it would undoubtedly affect your handling of all the other questions.

4) If the examination is of the essay type and contains but a few questions, it is a moot point as to whether you should read all the questions before starting to answer any one. Of course, if you are given a choice – say five out of seven and the like – then it is essential to read all the questions so you can eliminate the two that are most difficult. If, however, you are asked to answer all the questions, there may be danger in trying to answer the easiest one first because you may find that you will spend too much time on it. The best technique is to answer the first question, then proceed to the second, etc.

5) Time your answers. Before the exam begins, write down the time it started, then add the time allowed for the examination and write down the time it must be completed, then divide the time available somewhat as follows:

- If 3-1/2 hours are allowed, that would be 210 minutes. If you have 80 objective-type questions, that would be an average of 2-1/2 minutes per question. Allow yourself no more than 2 minutes per question, or a total of 160 minutes, which will permit about 50 minutes to review.
- If for the time allotment of 210 minutes there are 7 essay questions to answer, that would average about 30 minutes a question. Give yourself only 25 minutes per question so that you have about 35 minutes to review.

6) The most important instruction is to *read each question* and make sure you know what is wanted. The second most important instruction is to *time yourself properly* so that you answer every question. The third most important instruction is to *answer every question*. Guess if you have to but include something for each question. Remember that you will receive no credit for a blank and will probably receive some credit if you write something in answer to an essay question. If you guess a letter – say "B" for a multiple-choice question – you may have guessed right. If you leave a blank as an answer to a multiple-choice question, the examiners may respect your feelings but it will not add a point to your score. Some exams may penalize you for wrong answers, so in such cases *only*, you may not want to guess unless you have some basis for your answer.

7) Suggestions
   a. Objective-type questions
      1. Examine the question booklet for proper sequence of pages and questions
      2. Read all instructions carefully
      3. Skip any question which seems too difficult; return to it after all other questions have been answered
      4. Apportion your time properly; do not spend too much time on any single question or group of questions
      5. Note and underline key words – *all, most, fewest, least, best, worst, same, opposite,* etc.
      6. Pay particular attention to negatives
      7. Note unusual option, e.g., unduly long, short, complex, different or similar in content to the body of the question
      8. Observe the use of "hedging" words – *probably, may, most likely,* etc.
      9. Make sure that your answer is put next to the same number as the question
      10. Do not second-guess unless you have good reason to believe the second answer is definitely more correct
      11. Cross out original answer if you decide another answer is more accurate; do not erase until you are ready to hand your paper in
      12. Answer all questions; guess unless instructed otherwise
      13. Leave time for review

   b. Essay questions
      1. Read each question carefully
      2. Determine exactly what is wanted. Underline key words or phrases.
      3. Decide on outline or paragraph answer

4. Include many different points and elements unless asked to develop any one or two points or elements
5. Show impartiality by giving pros and cons unless directed to select one side only
6. Make and write down any assumptions you find necessary to answer the questions
7. Watch your English, grammar, punctuation and choice of words
8. Time your answers; don't crowd material

8) Answering the essay question

Most essay questions can be answered by framing the specific response around several key words or ideas. Here are a few such key words or ideas:

M's: manpower, materials, methods, money, management
P's: purpose, program, policy, plan, procedure, practice, problems, pitfalls, personnel, public relations
   a. Six basic steps in handling problems:
      1. Preliminary plan and background development
      2. Collect information, data and facts
      3. Analyze and interpret information, data and facts
      4. Analyze and develop solutions as well as make recommendations
      5. Prepare report and sell recommendations
      6. Install recommendations and follow up effectiveness

   b. Pitfalls to avoid
      1. *Taking things for granted* – A statement of the situation does not necessarily imply that each of the elements is necessarily true; for example, a complaint may be invalid and biased so that all that can be taken for granted is that a complaint has been registered
      2. *Considering only one side of a situation* – Wherever possible, indicate several alternatives and then point out the reasons you selected the best one
      3. *Failing to indicate follow up* – Whenever your answer indicates action on your part, make certain that you will take proper follow-up action to see how successful your recommendations, procedures or actions turn out to be
      4. *Taking too long in answering any single question* – Remember to time your answers properly

IX. AFTER THE TEST

Scoring procedures differ in detail among civil service jurisdictions although the general principles are the same. Whether the papers are hand-scored or graded by machine we have described, they are nearly always graded by number. That is, the person who marks the paper knows only the number – never the name – of the applicant. Not until all the papers have been graded will they be matched with names. If other tests, such as training and experience or oral interview ratings have been given, scores will be combined. Different parts of the examination usually have different weights. For example, the written test might count 60 percent of the final grade, and a rating of training and experience 40 percent. In many jurisdictions, veterans will have a certain number of points added to their grades.

After the final grade has been determined, the names are placed in grade order and an eligible list is established. There are various methods for resolving ties between those who get the same final grade – probably the most common is to place first the name of the person whose application was received first. Job offers are made from the eligible list in the order the names appear on it. You will be notified of your grade and your rank as soon as all these computations have been made. This will be done as rapidly as possible.

People who are found to meet the requirements in the announcement are called "eligibles." Their names are put on a list of eligible candidates. An eligible's chances of getting a job depend on how high he stands on this list and how fast agencies are filling jobs from the list.

When a job is to be filled from a list of eligibles, the agency asks for the names of people on the list of eligibles for that job. When the civil service commission receives this request, it sends to the agency the names of the three people highest on this list. Or, if the job to be filled has specialized requirements, the office sends the agency the names of the top three persons who meet these requirements from the general list.

The appointing officer makes a choice from among the three people whose names were sent to him. If the selected person accepts the appointment, the names of the others are put back on the list to be considered for future openings.

That is the rule in hiring from all kinds of eligible lists, whether they are for typist, carpenter, chemist, or something else. For every vacancy, the appointing officer has his choice of any one of the top three eligibles on the list. This explains why the person whose name is on top of the list sometimes does not get an appointment when some of the persons lower on the list do. If the appointing officer chooses the second or third eligible, the No. 1 eligible does not get a job at once, but stays on the list until he is appointed or the list is terminated.

X. HOW TO PASS THE INTERVIEW TEST

The examination for which you applied requires an oral interview test. You have already taken the written test and you are now being called for the interview test – the final part of the formal examination.

You may think that it is not possible to prepare for an interview test and that there are no procedures to follow during an interview. Our purpose is to point out some things you can do in advance that will help you and some good rules to follow and pitfalls to avoid while you are being interviewed.

What is an interview supposed to test?
The written examination is designed to test the technical knowledge and competence of the candidate; the oral is designed to evaluate intangible qualities, not readily measured otherwise, and to establish a list showing the relative fitness of each candidate – as measured against his competitors – for the position sought. Scoring is not on the basis of "right" and "wrong," but on a sliding scale of values ranging from "not passable" to "outstanding." As a matter of fact, it is possible to achieve a relatively low score without a single "incorrect" answer because of evident weakness in the qualities being measured.

Occasionally, an examination may consist entirely of an oral test – either an individual or a group oral. In such cases, information is sought concerning the technical knowledges and abilities of the candidate, since there has been no written examination for this purpose. More commonly, however, an oral test is used to supplement a written examination.

Who conducts interviews?

The composition of oral boards varies among different jurisdictions. In nearly all, a representative of the personnel department serves as chairman. One of the members of the board may be a representative of the department in which the candidate would work. In some cases, "outside experts" are used, and, frequently, a businessman or some other representative of the general public is asked to serve. Labor and management or other special groups may be represented. The aim is to secure the services of experts in the appropriate field.

However the board is composed, it is a good idea (and not at all improper or unethical) to ascertain in advance of the interview who the members are and what groups they represent. When you are introduced to them, you will have some idea of their backgrounds and interests, and at least you will not stutter and stammer over their names.

What should be done before the interview?

While knowledge about the board members is useful and takes some of the surprise element out of the interview, there is other preparation which is more substantive. It *is* possible to prepare for an oral interview – in several ways:

1) Keep a copy of your application and review it carefully before the interview

This may be the only document before the oral board, and the starting point of the interview. Know what education and experience you have listed there, and the sequence and dates of all of it. Sometimes the board will ask you to review the highlights of your experience for them; you should not have to hem and haw doing it.

2) Study the class specification and the examination announcement

Usually, the oral board has one or both of these to guide them. The qualities, characteristics or knowledges required by the position sought are stated in these documents. They offer valuable clues as to the nature of the oral interview. For example, if the job involves supervisory responsibilities, the announcement will usually indicate that knowledge of modern supervisory methods and the qualifications of the candidate as a supervisor will be tested. If so, you can expect such questions, frequently in the form of a hypothetical situation which you are expected to solve. NEVER go into an oral without knowledge of the duties and responsibilities of the job you seek.

3) Think through each qualification required

Try to visualize the kind of questions you would ask if you were a board member. How well could you answer them? Try especially to appraise your own knowledge and background in each area, *measured against the job sought*, and identify any areas in which you are weak. Be critical and realistic – do not flatter yourself.

4) Do some general reading in areas in which you feel you may be weak

For example, if the job involves supervision and your past experience has NOT, some general reading in supervisory methods and practices, particularly in the field of human relations, might be useful. Do NOT study agency procedures or detailed manuals. The oral board will be testing your understanding and capacity, not your memory.

5) Get a good night's sleep and watch your general health and mental attitude

You will want a clear head at the interview. Take care of a cold or any other minor ailment, and of course, no hangovers.

What should be done on the day of the interview?

Now comes the day of the interview itself. Give yourself plenty of time to get there. Plan to arrive somewhat ahead of the scheduled time, particularly if your appointment is in the fore part of the day. If a previous candidate fails to appear, the board might be ready for you a bit early. By early afternoon an oral board is almost invariably behind schedule if there are many candidates, and you may have to wait. Take along a book or magazine to read, or your application to review, but leave any extraneous material in the waiting room when you go in for your interview. In any event, relax and compose yourself.

The matter of dress is important. The board is forming impressions about you – from your experience, your manners, your attitude, and your appearance. Give your personal appearance careful attention. Dress your best, but not your flashiest. Choose conservative, appropriate clothing, and be sure it is immaculate. This is a business interview, and your appearance should indicate that you regard it as such. Besides, being well groomed and properly dressed will help boost your confidence.

Sooner or later, someone will call your name and escort you into the interview room. *This is it.* From here on you are on your own. It is too late for any more preparation. But remember, you asked for this opportunity to prove your fitness, and you are here because your request was granted.

What happens when you go in?

The usual sequence of events will be as follows: The clerk (who is often the board stenographer) will introduce you to the chairman of the oral board, who will introduce you to the other members of the board. Acknowledge the introductions before you sit down. Do not be surprised if you find a microphone facing you or a stenotypist sitting by. Oral interviews are usually recorded in the event of an appeal or other review.

Usually the chairman of the board will open the interview by reviewing the highlights of your education and work experience from your application – primarily for the benefit of the other members of the board, as well as to get the material into the record. Do not interrupt or comment unless there is an error or significant misinterpretation; if that is the case, do not hesitate. But do not quibble about insignificant matters. Also, he will usually ask you some question about your education, experience or your present job – partly to get you to start talking and to establish the interviewing "rapport." He may start the actual questioning, or turn it over to one of the other members. Frequently, each member undertakes the questioning on a particular area, one in which he is perhaps most competent, so you can expect each member to participate in the examination. Because time is limited, you may also expect some rather abrupt switches in the direction the questioning takes, so do not be upset by it. Normally, a board member will not pursue a single line of questioning unless he discovers a particular strength or weakness.

After each member has participated, the chairman will usually ask whether any member has any further questions, then will ask you if you have anything you wish to add. Unless you are expecting this question, it may floor you. Worse, it may start you off on an extended, extemporaneous speech. The board is not usually seeking more information. The question is principally to offer you a last opportunity to present further qualifications or to indicate that you have nothing to add. So, if you feel that a significant qualification or characteristic has been overlooked, it is proper to point it out in a sentence or so. Do not compliment the board on the thoroughness of their examination – they have been sketchy, and you know it. If you wish, merely say, "No thank you, I have nothing further to add." This is a point where you can "talk yourself out" of a good impression or fail to present an important bit of information. Remember, *you close the interview yourself.*

The chairman will then say, "That is all, Mr. _____, thank you." Do not be startled; the interview is over, and quicker than you think. Thank him, gather your belongings and take your leave. Save your sigh of relief for the other side of the door.

How to put your best foot forward

Throughout this entire process, you may feel that the board individually and collectively is trying to pierce your defenses, seek out your hidden weaknesses and embarrass and confuse you. Actually, this is not true. They are obliged to make an appraisal of your qualifications for the job you are seeking, and they want to see you in your best light. Remember, they must interview all candidates and a non-cooperative candidate may become a failure in spite of their best efforts to bring out his qualifications. Here are 15 suggestions that will help you:

1) Be natural – Keep your attitude confident, not cocky

If you are not confident that you can do the job, do not expect the board to be. Do not apologize for your weaknesses, try to bring out your strong points. The board is interested in a positive, not negative, presentation. Cockiness will antagonize any board member and make him wonder if you are covering up a weakness by a false show of strength.

2) Get comfortable, but don't lounge or sprawl

Sit erectly but not stiffly. A careless posture may lead the board to conclude that you are careless in other things, or at least that you are not impressed by the importance of the occasion. Either conclusion is natural, even if incorrect. Do not fuss with your clothing, a pencil or an ashtray. Your hands may occasionally be useful to emphasize a point; do not let them become a point of distraction.

3) Do not wisecrack or make small talk

This is a serious situation, and your attitude should show that you consider it as such. Further, the time of the board is limited – they do not want to waste it, and neither should you.

4) Do not exaggerate your experience or abilities

In the first place, from information in the application or other interviews and sources, the board may know more about you than you think. Secondly, you probably will not get away with it. An experienced board is rather adept at spotting such a situation, so do not take the chance.

5) If you know a board member, do not make a point of it, yet do not hide it

Certainly you are not fooling him, and probably not the other members of the board. Do not try to take advantage of your acquaintanceship – it will probably do you little good.

6) Do not dominate the interview

Let the board do that. They will give you the clues – do not assume that you have to do all the talking. Realize that the board has a number of questions to ask you, and do not try to take up all the interview time by showing off your extensive knowledge of the answer to the first one.

7) Be attentive

You only have 20 minutes or so, and you should keep your attention at its sharpest throughout. When a member is addressing a problem or question to you, give him your undivided attention. Address your reply principally to him, but do not exclude the other board members.

8) Do not interrupt

A board member may be stating a problem for you to analyze. He will ask you a question when the time comes. Let him state the problem, and wait for the question.

9) Make sure you understand the question

Do not try to answer until you are sure what the question is. If it is not clear, restate it in your own words or ask the board member to clarify it for you. However, do not haggle about minor elements.

10) Reply promptly but not hastily

A common entry on oral board rating sheets is "candidate responded readily," or "candidate hesitated in replies." Respond as promptly and quickly as you can, but do not jump to a hasty, ill-considered answer.

11) Do not be peremptory in your answers

A brief answer is proper – but do not fire your answer back. That is a losing game from your point of view. The board member can probably ask questions much faster than you can answer them.

12) Do not try to create the answer you think the board member wants

He is interested in what kind of mind you have and how it works – not in playing games. Furthermore, he can usually spot this practice and will actually grade you down on it.

13) Do not switch sides in your reply merely to agree with a board member

Frequently, a member will take a contrary position merely to draw you out and to see if you are willing and able to defend your point of view. Do not start a debate, yet do not surrender a good position. If a position is worth taking, it is worth defending.

14) Do not be afraid to admit an error in judgment if you are shown to be wrong

The board knows that you are forced to reply without any opportunity for careful consideration. Your answer may be demonstrably wrong. If so, admit it and get on with the interview.

15) Do not dwell at length on your present job

The opening question may relate to your present assignment. Answer the question but do not go into an extended discussion. You are being examined for a *new* job, not your present one. As a matter of fact, try to phrase ALL your answers in terms of the job for which you are being examined.

Basis of Rating

Probably you will forget most of these "do's" and "don'ts" when you walk into the oral interview room. Even remembering them all will not ensure you a passing grade. Perhaps you did not have the qualifications in the first place. But remembering them will help you to put your best foot forward, without treading on the toes of the board members.

Rumor and popular opinion to the contrary notwithstanding, an oral board wants you to make the best appearance possible. They know you are under pressure – but they also want to see how you respond to it as a guide to what your reaction would be under the pressures of the job you seek. They will be influenced by the degree of poise you display, the personal traits you show and the manner in which you respond.

ABOUT THIS BOOK

This book contains tests divided into Examination Sections. Go through each test, answering every question in the margin. At the end of each test look at the answer key and check your answers. On the ones you got wrong, look at the right answer choice and learn. Do not fill in the answers first. Do not memorize the questions and answers, but understand the answer and principles involved. On your test, the questions will likely be different from the samples. Questions are changed and new ones added. If you understand these past questions you should have success with any changes that arise. Tests may consist of several types of questions. We have additional books on each subject should more study be advisable or necessary for you. Finally, the more you study, the better prepared you will be. This book is intended to be the last thing you study before you walk into the examination room. Prior study of relevant texts is also recommended. NLC publishes some of these in our Fundamental Series. Knowledge and good sense are important factors in passing your exam. Good luck also helps. So now study this Passbook, absorb the material contained within and take that knowledge into the examination. Then do your best to pass that exam.

———

EXAMINATION SECTION

EXAMINATION SECTION
TEST 1

DIRECTIONS: Each question or incomplete statement is followed by several suggested answers or completions. Select the one the BEST answers the question or completes the statement. *PRINT THE LETTER OF THE CORRECT ANSWER IN THE SPACE AT THE RIGHT.*

1. Generally, slow learning is present in about _____% of people who suffer from Duchenne muscular dystrophy.
   A. 30
   B. 50
   C. 70
   D. 90

1._____

2. When a particular behavior reliably occurs only in the presence of certain stimulus events, the behavior is said to be
   A. generalized
   B. indiscriminate
   C. internalized
   D. under stimulus control

2._____

3. In the placement/training phase of a habilitation program, which of the following actions is associated with the agency's habilitation strategies?
   A. Employing effective prosthetic/accommodation techniques
   B. Gathering longitudinal data on clients
   C. Seeking integrated living arrangements
   D. Updating intersector working arrangements

3._____

4. Support and follow-up for transitional employment placements generally lasts for a period of
   A. 30 days
   B. 90 days
   C. 6 months
   D. 1 year

4._____

5. In the human brain, functions associated with sensation generally originate in the
   A. cerebellum
   B. septum
   C. occipital lobe
   D. parietal lobe

5._____

6. The habilitation specialist's attitude of trust and respect in the presence of a disabled client is know as the
   A. accommodation gesture
   B. protective stance
   C. equity posture
   D. authority position

6._____

7. Which of the following is <u>not</u> one of the primary goals noted in the Developmental Disabilities Assistance and Bill of Rights Act?

    A. Symptom alleviation
    B. Community integration
    C. Independence
    D. Productivity

7.____

8. The primary advantage associated with the use of functional definitions in relation to service delivery and program design is that these definitions

    A. increase the likelihood that a person with functional limitations will be classified as disabled
    B. simplify administrative tasks such as budgeting and resource allocation
    C. fit in with an established state and federal framework
    D. encourage the individualization of program planning on a person-by-person basis

8.____

9. Of the following areas of life activity, in which is a person with epilepsy LEAST likely to experience a deficit?

    A. Cognition
    B. Self-direction
    C. Economic self-sufficiency
    D. Independent living

9.____

10. Traditional techniques of behavior modification can be described as each of the following, <u>except</u>

    A. dynamic
    B. insight-oriented
    C. systematic
    D. focusing on the past

10.____

11. A person's overall life satisfaction is categorized as a(n) _____ quality of life factor.

    A. physical
    B. cognitive
    C. material
    D. social

11.____

12. Which of the following behavior treatment techniques is probably LEAST appropriate for affecting changes in the leisure skills of a mentally retarded client?

    A. Modeling
    B. Response contingent stimulation
    C. Physical prompts
    D. Verbal praise

12.____

13. Among mentally retarded persons, which of the following activities is likely to require the greatest degree of intervention and rehabilitation?

    A. Gross motor control
    B. Housekeeping

13.____

C. Eating
D. Grooming

14. Autistic clients can be reliably distinguished from nonautistic retarded clients of similar IQ or mental age on the basis of each of the following, <u>except</u>

    14.____

    A. cognitive test performance
    B. play patterns
    C. self-care
    D. language features

15. The goals of an individual habilitation plan include socialization, communication, and interaction. Which of the following instructional techniques will be most helpful?

    15.____

    A. Providing opportunities for decisions and choice
    B. Developing a stimulus-response chain based on task analysis
    C. Teaching generalization of social exchanges to other persons and settings
    D. Presenting multiple training examples within individual sessions

16. Which of the following is a diagnostic condition that is most likely to result in sensory/ neurological impairment?

    16.____

    A. Multiple sclerosis
    B. Hydrocephalus
    C. Epilepsy
    D. Cerebral palsy

17. Which of the following skill domains is relatively strong among clients with spina bifida?

    17.____

    A. Eye-hand coordination
    B. Mathematics
    C. Abstract reasoning
    D. Expressive language

18. Which of the following statements about generalized reinforcers is <u>false</u>?

    18.____

    A. Their use takes place in a naturally occurring learning environment.
    B. Satiation is rare due to the wide variety of reinforcers for which they can be exchanged
    C. They bridge the delay between the performance of the behavior and the receipt of additional reinforcers.
    D. They are easy to store and dispense.

19. In the human brain, functions associated with emotions and their expression generally originate in the

    19.____

    A. parietal lobe
    B. frontal lobe
    C. midbrain
    D. cerebellum

20. When selecting an instructional technique that will be effective with difficult-to-teach clients, it is important to choose the simplest possible successful strategy. The environmental components that need to be addressed include   20.___

    I.   the possible presence of some behavior that is incompatible with the task being taught
    II.   the presence or absence of necessary prerequisite skills
    III.   environmental stimuli such as the effectiveness of the instructions
    IV.   the motivational system

    A.   I and II
    B.   II, III and IV
    C.   III and IV
    D.   I, II, III and IV

21. In the past decade or so, employment services to the disabled have generally changed in each of the following ways, except a(n)   21.___

    A.   shift to public/private interfacing
    B.   shift to separate work facilities for groups of disabled workers
    C.   increased need for reportability focusing on person-referenced employment outcome data
    D.   increased need for on-site evaluation, training and habitation practices

22. Approximately what percentage of cases of mental retardation have primary biological and medical origins?   22.___

    A.   10
    B.   25
    C.   50
    D.   75

23. During play sessions in which a retarded child is being taught appropriate play behavior, the child's first correct toy-play response after an average of 5 minutes have elapsed is reinforced. This is an example of _____ reinforcement.   23.___

    A.   variable interval
    B.   fixed interval
    C.   variable ratio
    D.   fixed ratio

24. Three Amendments to the U.S. Constitution have played an essential role in social change as it affects adults with disabilities. Which of the following is not one of them?   24.___

    A.   Fifth
    B.   Eighth
    C.   Fourteenth
    D.   Sixteenth

25. Overcorrection is a behavior reduction technique that includes the two components of   25.____
    A.   response cost and modeling
    B.   fading and extinction
    C.   response cost and differential reinforcement
    D.   restitution and positive practice

KEY (CORRECT ANSWERS)

1.	C	11.	B
2.	D	12.	B
3.	A	13.	B
4.	C	14.	C
5.	D	15.	C
6.	C	16.	C
7.	A	17.	D
8.	D	18.	A
9.	A	19.	C
10.	C	20.	D

21.	B
22.	B
23.	A
24.	D
25.	D

TEST 2

DIRECTIONS: Each question or incomplete statement is followed by several suggested answers or completions. Select the one the BEST answers the question or completes the statement. *PRINT THE LETTER OF THE CORRECT ANSWER IN THE SPACE AT THE RIGHT.*

1. Which of the following is <u>not</u> an element of behavior analytic pre-vocational and vocational training?

    A. Acquisition, maintenance, and transfer
    B. Individualized training
    C. Qualitative description of behaviors
    D. Repeated assessments

1.____

2. According to the Developmental Disabilities Assistance and Bill of Rights Act, which of the following components is/are included in the definition of a severe and chronic "disability"?

    I.   It is attributable to a mental or physical impairment, or a combination of both
    II.   It reflects the person's need for a combination and sequence of special, interdisciplinary, or generic care, treatment, or other services
    III.   It results in substantial functional limitations
    IV.   It is attributable to substance dependence or adult-onset mental illness, or a combination of both

    A. I and II
    B. I, II and III
    C. I and IV
    D. I, II, III and IV

2.____

3. Which of the following is <u>not</u> a guideline that should be followed in the application of punishment to a developmentally disabled child?

    A. Avoid associating the delivery of punishment with the later delivery of reinforcement
    B. Apply punishment immediately following the behavior
    C. Punishment should be applied in graded steps
    D. Avoid prolonged or extensive use of punishment

3.____

4. Once a trainee has learned a new skill or reduced an inappropriate behavior, habilitation staff should consider the use of a(n)

    A. shaping sequence
    B. descriptive validation
    C. summative assessment
    D. intermittent schedule

4.____

5. In the human brain, functions associated with memory and the registration of new information generally originate in the

    A. parietal lobe
    B. temporal lobe

5.____

C. frontal lobe

D. hippocampus

6. The nutritional services offered to a person in a community contribute to the _____ of that person's quality of life.

A. physical

B. cognitive

C. material

D. social

6.____

7. The goals of an individual habilitation plan include generalization and mobility across environments. Which of the following instructional techniques will be most helpful?

A. Determining the appropriate modes of client communication

B. Sampling a range of relevant stimulus and response variation

C. Building learning activities on the client's interest

D. Simplifying the steps involved in a specific behavior

7.____

8. When using preference assessments for designing a habilitation program, each of the following is a guideline that should be followed, except

A. if activities are presented to the person, all should be presented several times in different combinations

B. program decisions should be made mostly on the basis of the personal interview

C. each type of assessment should be done over a period of days

D. equal attention should be paid to duration and quality of interactions

8.____

9. A client with muscular dystrophy is having difficulty feeding himself due to weakness in his arms. The first thing that should be tried is to

A. raise the table or eating surface a bit

B. fit the client with an elastic cuff that will hold a spoon

C. feed the client for a while and see if he will attempt to self-feed again

D. fit the client with special slings that will aid in feeding

9.____

10. Which of the following adaptations are most likely to be necessary for mentally retarded clients who take part in leisure activities?

A. Personal training

B. Environmental adaptations

C. Rule or procedural alterations

D. Material changes

10.____

11. Which of the following is an important consideration when developing a schedule of treatment sessions for an aphasic client?

A. Aphasia, once corrected, is often followed by a period of dysfluency

B. Aphasic persons communicate significantly better following periods of rest

C. The utterings of an aphasic client are usually part of a syndrome

D. Most aphasia is temporary

11.____

12. When a person leans to perform a desired response only in the presence of specific stimulus events, _____ occurred.

    A. generalization
    B. discrimination
    C. habituation
    D. shaping

12.____

13. When disabled workers lose their position in an integrated environment, it is usually because they

    A. were never very enthusiastic about the job
    B. have not been able to acquire the necessary skills
    C. did not receive adequate on-the-job support
    D. were unable to deal adequately with interpersonal issues

13.____

14. In behavioral modification, a generalized positive reinforcer may be exchanged by a client for a _____ reinforcer.

    A. conditioned
    B. negative
    C. backup
    D. contingent

14.____

15. A typical habilitation plan begins with a list of

    A. the client's goals as related to independence and integration
    B. the client's preferences and competencies
    C. a matching of the client with support services
    D. a summary of available resources

15.____

16. The primary disadvantage associated with the use of single-step behavior training is that the client

    A. is not aware of the ultimate goal of the behavior
    B. may experience difficulty transferring from skill training to the application session
    C. may not be provided with sufficient opportunities to practice discrimination
    D. does not have the opportunity to learn a skill intensively

16.____

17. Clients with _____ spina bifida are most likely to develop scoliosis.

    A. thoracic
    B. mid-lumbar
    C. lower lumbar
    D. sacral

17.____

18. Generally speaking, persons with a dual diagnosis are likely to be limited in life activity areas involving
    I. language
    II. independent living
    III. self-direction
    IV. learning

18.____

A. I and IV
B. II, III and IV
C. II and III
D. I, II, III and IV

19. When a client will perform a behavior better if she knows what the final product will be, which of the following instructional strategies is most appropriate?

    19.____

    A. Forward chaining
    B. Response cost
    C. Backward chaining
    D. Full-sequence training

20. Because of the limited amount of time generally available for behavioral skill instruction, habilitation workers generally make sure that the instruction is guided by each of the following principles, except

    20.____

    A. strategies should involve action by the client and observation by the instructor
    B. the instruction should focus on functional attributes
    C. improvements brought about by behaviors should all relate to the client's quality of life
    D. the skills taught should relate to the person's life-aim goals

21. When it occurs, a grand mal seizure usually lasts about

    21.____

    A. 10-15 seconds
    B. 30-60 seconds
    C. 2-5 minutes
    D. 5-7 minutes

22. Which of the following is common to virtually all language training programs for autistic or dual-diagnosis clients?

    22.____

    A. generalization
    B. teaching in small progressive steps
    C. segregation into phonemes and morphemes
    D. discrimination

23. Affective disorders are categorized as

    23.____

    A. anxiety disorders
    B. psychoses
    C. syndrome-associated conditions
    D. personality disorders

24. Which of the following is LEAST likely to be an area of deficit for a person with cerebral palsy?

    24.____

    A. Independent living
    B. Learning
    C. Self-direction
    D. Self-care

25. The focus of most community-living skills instruction programs for mentally retarded clients has tended to be   25.___

    A. telephone usage and money management
    B. language and socialization
    C. toileting and etiquette
    D. fire safety and mobility

_____

KEY (CORRECT ANSWERS)

1.	C		11.	B
2.	B		12.	B
3.	C		13.	D
4.	D		14.	C
5.	B		15.	B
6.	A		16.	B
7.	B		17.	A
8.	B		18.	B
9.	A		19.	C
10.	C		20.	A

21.	C
22.	B
23.	B
24.	C
25.	A

_____

EXAMINATION SECTION
TEST 1

DIRECTIONS: Each question or incomplete statement is followed by several suggested answers or completions. Select the one the BEST answers the question or completes the statement. *PRINT THE LETTER OF THE CORRECT ANSWER IN THE SPACE AT THE RIGHT.*

1. Mental retardation is primarily a(n) _____ concept.

    A. pharmaceutical
    B. psychological
    C. medical
    D. behavioral

1.____

2. Trends which currently impact service delivery in habilitation programs include each of the following, <u>except</u> a focus on

    A. outcomes and accountability
    B. the natural environment
    C. independent living in separate housing
    D. rights and empowerment of persons to make choices and decisions

2.____

3. In general, individual habilitation plans should be reviewed

    A. monthly
    B. every 6 months
    C. annually
    D. every 2 years

3.____

4. Which of the following is a diagnostic condition that is most likely to result in physical impairment?

    A. Down's syndrome
    B. Metabolic/immune deficiency disorder
    C. Arthrogryposis
    D. Bilateral blindness

4.____

5. A typical behavioral assessment concludes with a(n)

    A. ecological analysis
    B. contingency survey
    C. list of behavior parameters
    D. discussion of behavior change responsibility

5.____

6. Providing a client with work that is interesting, rewarding, and worthwhile is most likely to contribute to the _____ factors that foster well-being.

    A. physical
    B. material
    C. cognitive
    D. social

6.____

7. Of the following, probably the most significant trend affecting services for adults with dis-   7.____
abilities is

    A. evolving knowledge about particular medical or psychological conditions
    B. the involvement of family and friends
    C. the rise of the treatment/medical model
    D. the need for person-referenced outcomes

8. A 4-year-old autistic child who had just undergone cataract surgery needed to wear   8.____
glasses for nearly all of his waking hours, but consistently refused to do so, throwing
them aside whenever they were placed on his face. The habilitation staff decided to rein-
force the child's behavior in steps, rewarding him first for picking up his glasses, holding,
or carrying them; and then for wearing them for a few seconds at a time. Eventually, the
boy began to wear his glasses for 12 hours a day. The behavioral modification program
used by the staff in this case is an example of

    A. extinction
    B. shaping
    C. response priming
    D. negative reinforcement

9. Which of the following statements about transitional employment is <u>false</u>?   9.____

    A. Ongoing job-related supports are required by the disabled worker to maintain
       employment
    B. Extent of supports is flexible
    C. The work is in an environment where most people do not have disabilities
    D. Wages may be less than the prevailing or minimum rate

10. To teach an autistic client to use three-word utterances to label pictures or events, a   10.____
habilitation program should begin by helping the client to use _____.

    A. verb-adjective-noun
    B. negation in three words
    C. agent-action-object
    D. noun-verb-adverb

11. The two prime instructional strategies used in any behavior shaping program are   11.____

    A. discrimination and full-sequence training
    B. generalization and single-sequence training
    C. descriptive validation and response cost
    D. task analysis and instructional programming

12. Which of the following behavior reduction techniques generally involves the most punitive   12.____
strategies?

    A. overcorrection
    B. response contingent stimulation
    C. response cost
    D. differential reinforcement

13. Which of the following approaches would be most useful in assessing the behavior and characteristics of an inhabitant in a particular environment?

    A. Space coding
    B. Social ecology
    C. Organizational evaluation
    D. Person-environmental analysis

13.____

14. Approximately what percentage of all disabled U.S. adults are unemployed?

    A. 35
    B. 50
    C. 65
    D. 80

14.____

15. Sometimes, during the expressive language training of a mentally retarded adult, imitative verbal responses are not learned through modeling alone; often, imitation must be

    A. generalized across major response domains
    B. shaped with physical prompts
    C. taught after functional or spontaneous speech is acquired
    D. placed into the demand/response mode

15.____

16. Generally, the training of receptive language skills in mentally retarded clients has emphasized

    A. responses to sounds other than speech
    B. syntax
    C. verbal control of motor behavior
    D. reading aloud

16.____

17. Signs of tethering in a client with spina bifida include
    I. Back pain
    II. Pigeon-toed walk
    III. Progressive foot deformity
    IV. Spasticity

    A. I only
    B. I, III and IV
    C. II and IV
    D. I, II, III and IV

17.____

18. The use of intermittent reinforcement produces behavior that is

    A. easily produced upon demand
    B. more likely to produce satiation
    C. tends to be performed self-consciously
    D. more resistant to extinction

18.____

19. What is the term for a person's sense of where his/her body and limbs are in space?

    A. Kinesthesia
    B. Coordination

19.____

C. Proprioception
D. Dexterity

20. The federal law which states that all children with special needs should be placed in least restrictive environment possible is the

    20.___

    A. Americans with Disabilities Act (ADA)
    B. Developmental Disabilities Assistance and Bill of Rights Act
    C. Individuals with Disabilities Education Act (IDEA)
    D. Rehabilitation Act

21. A person's _____ originates with the fluid in the canals of the inner ear.

    21.___

    A. auricular
    B. proprioceptive
    C. tactile
    D. vestibular

22. When using the technique of a time-out from positive reinforcement in order to reduce a certain behavior, the most crucial consideration is

    22.___

    A. the type of behavior (language and posture) used by the professional to direct the client to the time-out area
    B. whether the client loses access to an environment that is reinforcing
    C. the frequency of the imposition of the time-out period
    D. the duration of the time-out period

23. In evaluating a habilitation program, which of the following contrasts a service's outcomes with those of a comparison group to determine whether the service made a difference?

    23.___

    A. Process analysis
    B. Outcome analysis
    C. Impact analysis
    D. Cost/benefit analysis

24. Which of the following is not common to all behavior modification techniques that are applied to meet the needs of disabled adults?

    24.___

    A. The ability to reproduce responses at will
    B. Reinforcement contingencies to alter the frequency of responses
    C. The identification of observable responses
    D. The measurement of responses over time

25. An individual habilitation plan should

    25.___

    I. identify which agency will provide each listed service
    II. have objectives stated in terms of emotional satisfaction
    III. always be in writing
    IV. include a statement of both short-term and long-term goals

A. I and II
B. I, III and IV
C. III and IV
D. I, II, III and IV

KEY (CORRECT ANSWERS)

1.	D		11.	D
2.	C		12.	B
3.	C		13.	D
4.	C		14.	C
5.	D		15.	B
6.	C		16.	C
7.	D		17.	B
8.	B		18.	D
9.	A		19.	A
10.	C		20.	C

21. D
22. B
23. C
24. A
25. B

TEST 2

DIRECTIONS: Each question or incomplete statement is followed by several suggested answers or completions. Select the one the BEST answers the question or completes the statement. *PRINT THE LETTER OF THE CORRECT ANSWER IN THE SPACE AT THE RIGHT.*

1. Each of the following statements about the social reinforcement of desired behaviors is true, except that it   1._____

    A. is naturally occurring
    B. is automatically reinforcing
    C. doesn't interrupt the performance of the behavior
    D. is very easy to administer

2. In the currently evolving mindset among habilitation professionals, the one common element seems to be   2._____

    A. an emphasis on self-sufficiency
    B. a refocusing of service delivery from diagnostic categories to individual needs
    C. a universal set of professional standards
    D. a set of fixed service delivery principles

3. The basic underlying deficit of autistic clients is a(n)   3._____

    A. inability to perform basic self-care functions such as eating and grooming
    B. lack of gross motor control
    C. inability to exist independently of caretakers
    D. severe receptive and expressive language impairment

4. Which of the following is most likely to be a secondary condition related to the primary effects of a disability?   4._____

    A. Learning disability
    B. Speech disorder
    C. Dystrophy
    D. Mental retardation

5. A person's self-help skills would most accurately be categorized as a(n) _____ of life factor.   5._____

    A. physical
    B. cognitive
    C. material
    D. social

6. Which of the following types of behavior treatment techniques is not widely used with clients who have a physical disability?   6._____

    A. Biofeedback
    B. Cognitive strategies
    C. Positive reinforcement
    D. Aversive control

7. Which of the following is a guideline that should be used in composing a client's behavioral outcomes?

    A. Specify the conditions under which the behavior will occur.
    B. Leave the date for final accomplishment open to allow for setbacks and adaptations.
    C. Avoid the use of contingency phrases
    D. Use the phrase "the client" or a suitable pronoun to avoid personalizing the objectives.

7.____

8. Which of the following is a diagnostic condition that is most likely to result in cognitive/developmental impairment?

    A. Fetal alcohol syndrome
    B. Spina bifida
    C. Hemiplegia
    D. Encephalocele

8.____

9. The main therapeutic goal for a hemiplegic client should be to

    A. teach the client to accomplish tasks with only one hand, by using substitutes for the other hand
    B. strengthen the leg of the weaker side
    C. outfit the client with the adequate number and type of prostheses that will be needed for basic self-care functions
    D. strengthen the arm of the weaker side

9.____

10. Research has shown that the prevalence of mental retardation corresponds with age, with sharp increases until about _____ and a marked decline after _____.

    A. 12;15
    B. 18; 21
    C. 25; 35
    D. 32; 45

10.____

11. A serious health hazard of severely mentally retarded clients is the ingestion of non-nutritive substances, known as

    A. mastication
    B. pica
    C. nostrum
    D. coprophagy

11.____

12. Among mentally retarded persons, which of the following activities is likely to require the greatest degree of intervention and rehabilitation?

    A. Language reception
    B. Socialization
    C. Hygiene
    D. Physical coordination

12.____

13. For teaching toileting skills to autistic or dual-diagnosis clients, the best approach is   13.____
probably to use a combination of

    A. modeling and faded guidance
    B. overcorrection and response contingent stimulation
    C. faded guidance and extinction
    D. positive reinforcement and overcorrection

14. Which of the following is LEAST likely to be a reason why a person with neuromuscular   14.____
impairment might exhibit symptoms of incontinence?

    A. Kidney infection
    B. Shyness or embarrassment at needing assistance to use the bathroom
    C. Bladder infection
    D. Sphincter weakness associated with the disease

15. Clients with high blood levels of anticonvulsants are likely to display any or all of the fol-   15.____
lowing side effects, except

    A. personality changes
    B. motor slowness
    C. auditory hallucinations
    D. reduced intellectual function

16. Which of the following movements is generally possible for a client with L2 spina bifida?   16.____

    A. Hip flexion
    B. Hip adduction
    C. Ankle plantarflexion
    D. Knee extension

17. A client receives reinforcement every fifth time he drinks from his cup without spilling.   17.____
This is an example of _____ reinforcement.

    A. variable interval
    B. fixed interval
    C. variable ratio
    D. fixed ratio

18. Which of the following is a field of language teaching that attempts to account for lan-   18.____
guage in terms of its uses in social contexts and discourse?

    A. Euphonies
    B. Pragmatics
    C. Mentalistics
    D. Sociolinguistics

19. A mentally-retarded client ruminates constantly throughout the day, despite verbal repri-   19.____
mands from habilitation staff. Probably the best approach to eliminating this behavior
would be to

    A. begin providing positive reinforcement
    B. provide large quantities of food and allow the client to consume as much as she
likes

C. ignore the behavior as much as possible
D. offer the client only two meals, supervised, each day

20. From a habilitation planning perspective, there are significant trends among persons whose primary diagnosis is either mental retardation, epilepsy, cerebral palsy, or dual diagnosis. Which of the following is <u>not</u> one of these?   20.____

    A. There are significant group differences in the mean level of assistance scores on learning
    B. There are few group differences in the level of economic self-sufficiency
    C. There are significant group differences in the ability to live independently
    D. There are few group differences in the level of self-care

21. For reducing the aggressive behaviors of autistic or dual-diagnosis clients, effective approaches include   21.____
    I. generalized positive reinforcement
    II. time-outs
    III. extinction
    IV. response contingent stimulation

    A. I and II
    B. II, III and IV
    C. III and IV
    D. I, II, III and IV

22. The federal law that requires an Individualized Education Plan (IEP) for school children who qualify for special education and related services is the   22.____

    A. Americans with Disabilities Act (ADA)
    B. Developmental Disabilities Assistance and Bill of Rights Act
    C. Individuals with Disabilities Education Act (IDEA)
    D. Rehabilitation Act

23. Of the following areas of life activity, adults diagnosed as mentally retarded are LEAST likely to have deficits in the area of   23.____

    A. language
    B. self-direction
    C. economic self-sufficiency
    D. learning

24. For a young client with spina bifida, clean intermittent catheterization (CIC) should be performed _____ a day.   24.____

    A. once
    B. twice
    C. 3 or 4 times
    D. 5 or 6 times

25. Each of the following is a disadvantage associated with the use of categorical or diag-   25.___
nostic definitions in relation to service delivery and program design, <u>except</u>

    A. difficulty determining a general set of disabilities that need to be addressed
    B. overly rigid adherence to exclusionary policies
    C. insufficient acknowledgement of individual differences within a category
    D. lack of sensitivity in evaluation instruments

KEY (CORRECT ANSWERS)

1.	B		11.	B
2.	B		12.	B
3.	D		13.	D
4.	B		14.	D
5.	D		15.	C
6.	B		16.	B
7.	A		17.	D
8.	A		18.	B
9.	A		19.	B
10.	A		20.	A

21.	C
22.	D
23.	A
24.	D
25.	A

EXAMINATION SECTION
TEST 1

DIRECTIONS: Each question or incomplete statement is followed by several suggested answers or completions. Select the one the BEST answers the question or completes the statement PRINT THE LETTER OF THE CORRECT ANSWER IN THE SPACE AT THE RIGHT.

1. Each of the following is a disadvantage associated with the use of functional definitions in relation to service delivery and program design, except

    A. lack of refinement in the key elements of definitions
    B. inattention to the assets of individual persons
    C. general lack of clarity
    D. increased likelihood that a person needing assistance may not be classified as disabled

1.____

2. Which of the following is a factor which contributes directly to a person's capacity for self-direction?

    A. Vocational skills
    B. Grooming
    C. Socialization
    D. Academic skills

2.____

3. The principle of normalization defines five accomplishments that define effective habilitation services. These include each of the following, except

    A. community presence
    B. status improvement
    C. competence development
    D. economic self-sufficiency

3.____

4. When determining a specific intervention strategy for a client, which of the following steps is usually performed first?

    A. Prioritizing interventions on the basis of the person's need to feel safe and successful
    B. Determining what skills will be needed and what challenges will be addressed
    C. Using person-environment assessment information to determine mismatches
    D. Determining whether behavioral skill training, prosthetics, or environmental accommodation will be used

4.____

5. Which of the following classifiers would be used in an ecological description of a person's environment?

    A. Physical design
    B. Procedures
    C. Demographics
    D. Personal development

5.____

6. Which of the following type of seizures is defined as an episode of inappropriate or pur-   6._____
poseless behavior, with subsequent amnesia regarding the episode?

    A. Tourette's
    B. Petit mal
    C. Psychomotor
    D. Grand mal

7. Most experience with disabled learners supports the proposition that teaching the   7._____
_____ function of language will enhance the acquisition of a broader vocabulary.

    A. receptive
    B. instrumental
    C. emotional
    D. symbolic

8. Which of the following factors may produce cerebral palsy?   8._____
    I. Congenital factors
    II. Injury
    III. Disease

    A. I only
    B. I and II
    C. I and III
    D. I, II, and III

9. Typically, a behavioral objective written for a client will <u>first</u> list   9._____

    A. a qualitative description of the desired behavior
    B. the criterion for success
    C. the observable outcome
    D. the target date for the trainee's accomplishment of the outcome.

10. A habilitation program involves a training regimen for teaching spinal cord-injured clients   10._____
to do wheelchair push-ups in order to prevent pressure sores: a 30-second alarm sounds
if the client has not done a 4-second push-up during a 10-minute interval. The alarm
could be postponed at any time during the 10-minute interval by doing a push-up. This is
an example of

    A. aversive control
    B. extinction
    C. fixed rate reinforcement
    D. stimulus control

11. To teach an autistic client to respond to questions, a habilitation program begins by help-   11._____
ing the client answer yes/no questions. Typically, the instructor and the client would then
focus on _____ questions.

    A. why
    B. who
    C. how
    D. where

12. Which of the following is a behavior that would typically require only intermittent rein-forcement?

    A. A mentally retarded client drinking from a cup
    B. A retarded client dressing appropriately each morning
    C. A client with cerebral palsy climbing into a swing on the playground
    D. A client with cerebral palsy turning on a stereo

12.____

13. Which of the following developmental disabilities generally involves the greatest risk for obesity?

    A. Cerebral palsy
    B. Spina bifida
    C. Down syndrome
    D. Muscular dystrophy

13.____

14. Under federal law, if a program receives money from the government, it is required to allow individuals with disabilities to participate. This is a provision of section 504 of the

    A. Americans with Disabilities Act (ADA)
    B. Developmental Disabilities Assistance and Bill of Rights Act
    C. Individuals with Disabilities Education Act (IDEA)
    D. Rehabilitation Act

14.____

15. An autistic child is constantly picking up objects and putting them in his mouth. In order to reduce this behavior, the habilitation staff began a program of oral hygiene training in which the child brushed his gums with oral antiseptic and wiped his lips with a washcloth soaked in antiseptic. The frequency of this training reduced in measure with the child's placement of objects in his mouth. This is an example of the use of the behavior reduc-tion technique known as

    A. extinction
    B. response contingent stimulation
    C. differential reinforcement of low rates of behavior
    D. overcorrection

15.____

16. In establishing an expressive speech system in a mentally retarded client, the first phase of a habilitation program usually involves

    A. imitation training
    B. instruction-followed behaviors
    C. reading aloud
    D. pronoun use

16.____

17. Which of the following is categorized as a psychosis?

    A. Conversion reaction
    B. Antisocial personality
    C. Adjustment disorder
    D. Schizophrenia

17.____

18. Which of the following is <u>not</u> a general guideline that should be followed when adapting recreation/leisure activities as part of a habilitation plan?

    A. Procedural adaptations should be tried before any other
    B. Any adaptation should be considered temporary
    C. Inexpensive and portable adaptations should be tried first
    D. No adaptation should be attempted until task assessment and instruction indicate that the person cannot learn the activity through conventional teaching strategies

18.____

19. The determinant in an interval schedule of behavior reinforcement is

    A. the likeness of the behavior to its established target
    B. the quantity of the behavior
    C. the passage of time since the last reinforcer was delivered
    D. the rate of performance of the behavior

19.____

20. Habilitation professionals propose that a person's quality of life increases as one's access to culturally typical activities and settings increases. This is known as the principle of

    A. the least-restrictive environment
    B. normalization
    C. autonomy
    D. Gestalt

20.____

21. Signs of intoxication of the major anticonvulsants include
    I. irritability
    II. dysarthria (poorly articulated speech)
    III. ataxia
    IV. aphasia

    A. I only
    B. I, II and III
    C. III and IV
    D. I, II, III and IV

21.____

22. In relation to community living programs, the focus of a residential living decision should generally be directed to each of the following, <u>except</u>

    A. presence of friends in the neighborhood
    B. personal preference for living situation
    C. preparation for normal adult living
    D. proximity to family

22.____

23. In general, high rates of _____ behavior occupy a disproportionate status in the repertoires of autistic and other severely impaired clients.

    A. aggressive
    B. self-destructive
    C. oversexualized
    D. self-stimulatory

23.____

24. According to D'Zurilla and Nezu, the problem-solving process begins with   24.____

    A. verification of the problem
    B. the generation of alternatives
    C. problem definition and formulation
    D. general orientation

25. Developmentally disabled clients frequently exhibit repetitious movements that occur at a   25.____
high rate and have no apparent adaptive function. These behaviors are described as

    A. inconsequential
    B. stereotyped
    C. rumination
    D. ritualistic

KEY (CORRECT ANSWERS)

1.	B		11.	B
2.	C		12.	B
3.	D		13.	B
4.	B		14.	D
5.	A		15.	D
6.	C		16.	A
7.	B		17.	D
8.	B		18.	A
9.	C		19.	C
10.	A		20.	B

21.	B
22.	C
23.	D
24.	D
25.	B

TEST 2

DIRECTIONS: Each question or incomplete statement is followed by several suggested answers or completions. Select the one the BEST answers the question or completes the statement. *PRINT THE LETTER OF THE CORRECT ANSWER IN THE SPACE AT THE RIGHT.*

1. Definitions used in the field of habilation are used for
    I. planning
    II. policy development
    III. establishing eligibility

    A. I and II
    B. I and III
    C. III only
    D. I, II and III

1.____

2. In _____% of mentally retarded individuals with an IQ of less than 50, there is an absence or near absence of speech.

    A. 15-35
    B. 35-45
    C. 55-65
    D. 75-85

2.____

3. In a typical habilitation plan documentation format, which of the following elements appears last?

    A. Service plan
    B. Current life-aim goals
    C. Discussions with the client and family
    D. Interdisciplinary recommendations

3.____

4. Which of the following is not considered to be an element of a person's psychosocial climate?

    A. Relationship
    B. Physical location
    C. Systems maintenance/change
    D. Personal development

4.____

5. All discrimination training begins with the

    A. formulation of behavioral objectives
    B. initiation of full-sequence training
    C. establishment of a predictable relationship between a cue and a response
    D. initiation of discrimination training

5.____

6. The primary visual cortex of the human brain is located in the _____ lobe.

    A. frontal
    B. parietal
    C. temporal
    D. occipital

6.____

7. The first step in a typical behavioral assessment is a(n)   7.____

    A. list of behavior parameters
    B. contingency survey
    C. detailed history
    D. ecological analysis

8. Approximately what percentage of people with cerebral palsy have a normal intelligence?   8.____

    A. 20
    B. 40
    C. 60
    D. 80

9. Which of the following statements about Duchenne muscular dystrophy is false?   9.____

    A. It involves a longer life expectancy than other forms of MD
    B. It is usually not apparent until a child begins to walk
    C. It eventually ends in wheelchair confinement
    D. It affects only males

10. The goals of an individual habilitation plan include motivation and participation fluency. Which of the following instructional techniques will be most helpful?   10.____

    A. Developing a stimulus-response chain
    B. Presenting multiple training examples within individual sessions
    C. Prompting and reinforcing targeted social interactions and sequences
    D. Using an effective balance of demand and reward

11. In evaluating a habilitation program, which of the following provides objective person-referenced data sets reflecting changes in the person's living skills, employment efforts, and community integration?   11.____

    A. Process analysis
    B. Outcome analysis
    C. Impact analysis
    D. Cost/benefit analysis

12. Which of the following is an objective measure of a client's quality of life?   12.____

    A. Friendships
    B. Relations with other people
    C. Recreation
    D. Appearance/physical condition

13. The most common speech disorder among clients with neurological impairments is   13.____

    A. dysfluency (stuttering)
    B. echolalia
    C. cri-du-chat
    D. aphasia

14. Disadvantages associated with the traditional pre-employment assessment of clients include   14.____
   I.   assessments all take place in isolation from a true work environment
   II. results that tend to limit rather than expand the client's opportunities
   III. evaluations don't include an inquiry into client's interest
   IV. an inability to measure specific sets of skills

   A. I, II and III
   B. II and IV
   C. III only
   D. I, II, III and IV

15. An adult client with mild mental retardation is doing a set of math problems. The instructor, on average, praises the client after every fifth completed itemsometimes after four items or nine items. This schedule, which produces a stable and high rate of behavior, is known as _____ reinforcement.   15.____

   A. variable interval
   B. fixed interval
   C. variable ratio
   D. fixed ratio

16. For teaching self-help skills to autistic or dual-diagnosis clients, the best approach is probably to use a combination of   16.____

   A. backward chaining and faded guidance
   B. extinction and positive reinforcement
   C. differential reinforcement of other behaviors (DRO) and response contingent stimulation
   D. faded guidance and overcorrection

17. In the teaching of attention and listening skills, "attention" is often defined as one or more of the following, <u>except</u>   17.____

   A. on-task behavior
   B. posture
   C. silence
   D. eye contact

18. In athetoid cerebral palsy,   18.___

   A. muscle tone is constantly changing
   B. a person has severe balance and coordination but is usually ambulatory
   C. only one side of the body is affected
   D. joints are consistently stiffened

19. A worker is attempting to teach a client to cross an uncontrolled intersection. The worker begins with a verbal prompt to walk to the curb and stop, but the trainee fails to do this. The worker than says, "Watch me, I'm going to walk to the curb and stop." This is an example of   19.___

   A. physical prompting
   B. task analysis

    C.   graduated guidance
    D.   summative assessment

20. Each of the following types of behaviors are generally included in the professional defini-   20.____
tion of "emotional disturbance," <u>except</u> those that

    A.   markedly deviate from age-appropriate expectations
    B.   interfere with positive personal and interpersonal development
    C.   are considered socially unacceptable
    D.   are culturally specific

21. In accordance with the principle of the least restrictive environment for a disabled client   21.____
in treatment, one of the first types of strategies that should be attempted in a behavior
reduction program is

    A.   overcorrection
    B.   response contingent stimulation
    C.   response cost
    D.   differential reinforcement

22. Which of the following is an instructional strategy that make use of task analysis?   22.____

    A.   Response cost
    B.   Extinction
    C.   Overcorrection
    D.   Backward chaining

23. The principles to be instituted in a community living program include   23.____
    I.   guidance by personal reference outcomes
    II.   the teaching of functional skills
    III.   a regeneration of the community
    IV.   a focus on behavior control

    A.   I and II
    B.   I, II and III
    C.   III and IV
    D.   I, II, III and IV

24. Clients with hemiplegia could generally perform well at each of the following occupations,   24.____
<u>except</u>

    A.   dispatcher
    B.   shipping clerk
    C.   small engine repair
    D.   receptionist

25. The factor which distinguishes overcorrection from other behavior reduction techniques   25.____
is that it

    A.   can be administered in a nonemotional manner
    B.   teaches alternate desirable behaviors
    C.   is used to suppress self-injurious behaviors
    D.   inflicts a form of punishment on the client

KEY (CORRECT ANSWERS)

1.	D		11.	B
2.	D		12.	D
3.	C		13.	D
4.	B		14.	A
5.	C		15.	C
6.	D		16.	A
7.	C		17.	C
8.	B		18.	A
9.	A		19.	C
10.	D		20.	D

21. D
22. D
23. B
24. C
25. B

———

EXAMINATION SECTION
TEST 1

DIRECTIONS: Each question or incomplete statement is followed by several suggested answers or completions. Select the one the BEST answers the question or completes the statement. *PRINT THE LETTER OF THE CORRECT ANSWER IN THE SPACE AT THE RIGHT.*

1. From a habitation planning perspective, there are significant trends among persons whose primary diagnosis is either mental retardation, epilepsy, cerebral palsy, or dual diagnosis. These trends include

   A. less need among epileptics for assistance in language
   B. more need among mentally retarded persons for assistance in mobility
   C. significant group differences in the mean level of assistance scores on self-direction
   D. generally insignificant need among all groups for assistance in independent living

1.____

2. Any procedure that encourages a client to engage in the early steps of a sequence of behaviors is referred to as

   A. response priming
   B. prompting
   C. impulsion
   D. shaping

2.____

3. From a habilitation standpoint, quality of life is

   A. the outcome of individuals meeting basic needs in private
   B. basically an intrapersonal phenomenon and a product of self-perception
   C. defined by the consumer rather than the professional
   D. different for persons with and without disabilities

3.____

4. Which of the following conditions is produced only by congenital factors?

   A. Muscular dystrophy
   B. Epilepsy
   C. Myelomeningocele
   D. Cerebral palsy

4.____

5. The environmental assessment known as space coding is used to evaluate a(n)

   A. person's functional reinforcements
   B. person's behavioral setting
   C. organizational structure
   D. psychosocial climate

5.____

6. In adults, the diagnostic correlative to autism is known as

   A. dual diagnosis
   B. gross dysfunction
   C. apathy
   D. antisocial disorder

6.____

7. Which of the following is a behavior reduction procedure?

    A. Fading
    B. Response priming
    C. Extinction
    D. Shaping

7.____

8. Which of the following is a diagnostic condition that is most likely to result in emotional/behavioral impairment?

    A. Autism
    B. Anencephalus
    C. Cerebral palsy
    D. Traumatic brain injury

8.____

9. In general, a wheelchair-bound client with neuromuscular impairment should be bathed

    A. daily
    B. every other day
    C. twice weekly
    D. weekly

9.____

10. In the maintenance phase of a habilitation program, which of the following actions is associated with the agency's systems interface?

    A. Environmental assessments of necessary skills
    B. Altering or preserving interagency and intersector working agreements
    C. Committing resources to placement
    D. Allocation of staff to long-term supports

10.____

11. Which of the following is not a component of the limbic system?

    A. Hypothalamus
    B. Amygdala
    C. Pons
    D. Hippocampus

11.____

12. Which of the following conditions is likely to produce a neurological handicap?

    A. Amputation
    B. Muscular dystrophy
    C. Arthritis
    D. Epilepsy

12.____

13. For a client with cerebral palsy, ataxia will generally continue to improve until the age of approximately _____, at which time balance and coordination systems will reach maximum improvement.

    A. 8-10
    B. 12-15
    C. 15-18
    D. 19-25

13.____

14. Children with Down syndrome typically suffer from each of the following physical problems, __except__   14.____

    A. short limbs
    B. low muscle strength
    C. hypertonia
    D. high joint flexibility

15. Of the following skills, which would typically be taught to an autistic client first?   15.____

    A. Labeling objects and events using simple sentences
    B. Appropriate pronoun usage
    C. Responding to questions
    D. The use of two-word utterances to label pictures or events

16. Which of the following statements concerning an individual habilitation plan is true?   16.____

    A. It should be developed individually by the habilitation specialist
    B. It should name the agency that will provide the service, and then leave personnel assignments up to that agency
    C. A specific evaluation procedure and schedule for determining the achievement of objectives should be included in the plan
    D. Parents or guardians of clients should only be shown the plan after it has been written

17. Most language programs used in habilitation involve a behavioral approach to the acquisition of symbols and words known as   17.____

    A. phonics
    B. discrimination training
    C. gradual articulation
    D. whole language

18. Research has shown that the best way to teach emergency telephone skills to mentally retarded clients is to   18.____

    A. downplay the importance of the skill as it relates to their well-being
    B. integrate lessons into a generalized unit of telephone skills
    C. divide each emergency call into a series of sub-tasks
    D. conduct simulations that are as much like real emergencies as possible

19. What type of cerebral palsy is characterized by abnormally high muscle tone, tight or stiff muscle joints, and limited movement in affected areas?   19.____

    A. Diplegic
    B. Athetoid
    C. Ataxic
    D. Spastic

20. Which of the following is a social indicator of a community's quality of life?   20.____

    A. Material well-being
    B. Residential arrangement

C. Leisure
D. Psychological well-being

21. In the pre-vocational and vocational training of mentally retarded clients, which of the fol- 21.___
lowing forms of instructor assistance is generally most desirable?

A. Physical assistance
B. Modeling
C. Physical prompting
D. Verbal cue

22. Which of the following is not a transitional-situational disorder? 22.___

A. Conversion reaction
B. Adjustment reaction
C. Suicide gestures
D. Symptomatic alcoholism

23. For reducing the self-stimulatory behaviors of autistic or dual-diagnosis clients, effective 23.___
approaches include
    I. overcorrection
    II. time-outs
    III. extinction
    IV. punishment

A. I and II
B. I and IV
C. II, III and IV
D. III and IV

24. Which of the following skill domains is relatively weak among clients with spina bifida? 24.___

A. Long-term memory
B. Writing
C. Spelling
D. Social cognition

25. A therapist used physical prompts to teach sign language to several profoundly retarded, 25.___
autistic children. Training consisted of the therapist holding up an item (e.g., an apple)
while saying "apple." If the child failed to make the sign for apple, the therapist guided the
child's hand into the correct sign while repeating "apple." Once the child made the correct
sign, reinforcement was provided. Eventually, the therapist provided less help to the child
until the sign was made without assistance.
This case illustrates the use of the technique of

A. fading
B. extinction
C. differential reinforcement of other behavior
D. response priming

KEY (CORRECT ANSWERS)

1.	A		11.	C
2.	A		12.	D
3.	C		13.	A
4.	C		14.	C
5.	B		15.	D
6.	A		16.	C
7.	C		17.	B
8.	A		18.	C
9.	A		19.	D
10.	B		20.	C

21. D
22. A
23. B
24. B
25. A

———

TEST 2

DIRECTIONS: Each question or incomplete statement is followed by several suggested answers or completions. Select the one the BEST answers the question or completes the statement. *PRINT THE LETTER OF THE CORRECT ANSWER IN THE SPACE AT THE RIGHT.*

1. For teaching specific competencies such as cognition and physical movements, one of the most useful instructional techniques would probably be to   1.____

   A. use a wide range of relevant stimulus and response variation
   B. conduct mass trials
   C. focus initially on demand more than reward
   D. present multiple training examples within individual sessions

2. The new behavioral/training technology used in habilitation programs focuses on the person-environmental perspective, and has each of the following characteristics, <u>except</u>   2.____

   A. environments are best described in terms of global names or functions, rather than specific demand characteristics
   B. the behavioral and competency requirements of environments can be objectively and reliably assessed
   C. personal and environmental attributes can be compared and discrepancies identified
   D. persons can be accurately described in terms of a set of concrete and measurable attributes

3. A number of agency-level factors are critical to an effective and efficient habilitation program. Which of the following factors includes the approaches used to assess an adult with disabilities on relevant performance requirements?   3.____

   A. Systems interface
   B. Habilitation strategies
   C. Natural environment
   D. Agency characteristics

4. In the human brain, functions associated with planning, initiating, and organizing generally originate in the   4.____

   A. amygdala
   B. occipital lobe
   C. frontal lobe
   D. pons

5. Overcorrection is a behavior reduction technique that   5.____

   A. requires fewer staff than other procedures generally do
   B. avoids physical or manual guidance
   C. is designed only to reduce problem behavior
   D. generally requires one-to-one supervision

6. In a typical habilitation plan documentation format, which of the following elements appears first?

    A. Interdisciplinary recommendations
    B. Existing prosthetics and environmental modifications
    C. Review of previous life-aim goals
    D. Service plan

6._____

7. A young client with myelomeningocele and a resulting neurogenic bladder should generally be expected to self-catheterize by around the age of

    A. 3 or 4
    B. 6 or 7
    C. 9 or 10
    D. 12 or 13

7._____

8. Which of the following skills are generally common to all types of habilitation curricula?

    A. living/work/recreation skills
    B. language
    C. social skills
    D. problem-solving/decision making

8._____

9. As quality-of-life measures, social indicators can accurately represent
    I. the collective quality of community life
    II. an individual's perceived quality of life
    III. outcomes from rehabilitation programs

    A. I only
    B. I and II
    C. II and III
    D. I, II and III

9._____

10. The main obstacle to the teaching of self-feeding skills to developmentally disabled clients is the

    A. infrequency of learning opportunities
    B. lack of social reference points or consequences for specified behaviors
    C. ethical problems inherent in the use of food as a reinforcement
    D. need for physical agility

10._____

11. A habilitation worker is training a client in the presence of a second trainer who will later assist the client's later efforts to work on the same task. This is a simple example of

    A. stimulus control
    B. generalization
    C. discrimination
    D. forward chaining

11._____

12. What is the behavioral term for the procedure used to teach successive approximations to a complex target behavior, until the client is able to perform the complete behavior?

    A. Chunking
    B. Overcorrection

12._____

    C.   Shaping
    D.   Normalization

13.   Which of the following muscle groups will generally be most important for a client with   13.____
        T12 spina bifida?

    A.   Glutei
    B.   Gastrocs
    C.   Hip flexors
    D.   Anterior tibials

14.   For adults with disabilities, Title _____ the Social Security Act delineates the mainte-   14.____
        nance program that is most likely to be used.

    A.   II
    B.   VII
    C.   IX
    D.   XVI

15.   The specific diagnostic criteria for infantile autism include   15.____
            I.   Peculiar speech patterns
           II.   Delusions
          III.   Onset before 30 months of age

    A.   I only
    B.   I and III
    C.   II and III
    D.   I, II, and III

16.   Which of the following is a subjective measure of a client's quality of life?   16.____

    A.   Available services
    B.   Education
    C.   Mobility
    D.   Competence/productivity

17.   Because of the complex difficulties involved in teaching or reducing the behaviors of   17.____
        developmentally disabled clients, which of the following techniques is generally most lim-
        ited in it application among habilitation programs?

    A.   Fading
    B.   Overcorrection
    C.   Response contingent stimulation
    D.   Extinction

18.   Which of the following is <u>not</u> a category in the Autism Behavior Checklist, the first compo-   18.____
        nent of the Autism Screening Instrument for Educational Planning (ASIEP)?

    A.   Sensory
    B.   Body and object use
    C.   Language
    D.   Associative

19. Which of the following is categorized as an anxiety disorder?   19.____

    A. Conversion reaction
    B. Adjustment reaction
    C. Lesch-Nyan syndrome
    D. Antisocial personality

20. A client is introduced to an integrated employment environment. If she is placed in com-   20.____
    petitive employment,

    A. most of the workers in her workplace or department will be disabled
    B. her wages will be at or above the prevailing or minimum rate
    C. whatever supports are provided will be at the job site
    D. she will not require ongoing job-related supports

21. A workshop instructor wants to increase the attentiveness of a 10-year-old child with mild   21.____
    mental retardation. With the help of an aide, the instructor reinforces the first occurrence
    of attentive behavior that occurs after 1 minute of the behavior has elapsed. This is an
    example of _____ reinforcement.

    A. variable interval
    B. fixed interval
    C. variable ratio
    D. fixed ratio

22. The most common functional disabilities resulting from a traumatic brain injury include   22.____
    I.   Motor disturbances
    II. Fatigue
    III. Difficulty in maintaining concentration
    IV. Altered control and expression of emotions

    A. I and III
    B. I, III and IV
    C. I, III and IV
    D. I, II, III and IV

23. When used as a behavior reduction strategy, a response contingent stimulus should be   23.____
    each of the following, except

    A. strong enough to suppress the behavior
    B. consistently applied to every occurrence of the behavior
    C. begin as mildly as possible, and then increase in intensity
    D. applied immediately following the undesired behavior

24. Which of the following approaches is used to assess a client's psychosocial climate?   24.____

    A. Systems maintenance analysis
    B. Social ecology
    C. Space coding
    D. Physical setting analysis

25. Which of the following is characterized as a generalized positive reinforcer?   25.____

    A. A smile
    B. Food
    C. Praise
    D. Money

———

KEY (CORRECT ANSWERS)

1.	B		11.	B
2.	A		12.	C
3.	B		13.	C
4.	C		14.	D
5.	D		15.	B
6.	A		16.	A
7.	B		17.	D
8.	D		18.	D
9.	A		19.	A
10.	A		20.	B

21.	B
22.	D
23.	C
24.	B
25.	D

EXAMINATION SECTION
TEST 1

DIRECTIONS: Each question or incomplete statement is followed by several suggested answers or completions. Select the one that BEST answers the question or completes the statement. *PRINT THE LETTER OF THE CORRECT ANSWER IN THE SPACE AT THE RIGHT.*

1. Which of the following statements is TRUE?   1.____

    A. The goal of normalization is to allow one to do whatever one likes.
    B. Normalization involves making a person become normal.
    C. Normalization advocates that whenever possible, people's perceptions of developmentally disabled individuals must be enhanced or improved.
    D. Normalization advocates encouraging the developmentally disabled to be just like everyone else.

2. It is important to view the developmentally disabled as   2.____

    A. helpless
    B. unable to make decisions
    C. deviant
    D. none of the above

3. All of the following would be considered good practice EXCEPT   3.____

    A. providing residential services in the community, rather than in an isolated area
    B. placing residential homes next to rural prisons
    C. providing access in residences to accommodate those who are non-ambulatory
    D. avoiding excessive rules that tend to separate staff from residents

4. All of the following are true in normalization EXCEPT   4.____

    A. family involvement in normalization is usually not helpful to achieving the goal
    B. clients should be involved, when possible, in selecting programming in order to develop independence
    C. program options should emphasize autonomy, independence, integration, and productivity
    D. it is a good idea when possible to have day programming located apart from the living setting

5. Benefits of normalization include all of the following EXCEPT   5.____

    A. development of self-confidence and self-esteem in the developmentally disabled
    B. social integration of the developmentally disabled
    C. positive changes in societal attitudes regarding the developmentally disabled
    D. societal acceptance of deviance

6. All of the following statements are true EXCEPT: 6.____

    A. Normalization means that normal conditions of life should be made available to developmentally disabled people
    B. Attitudes toward the mentally retarded have a great effect on the way they are treated, and, consequently, on their chances for living a productive, normal life

C. It is highly unlikely that efforts at normalization will succeed in most communities

D. What is normal or typical in one society may not be normal or typical in another

7. In normalization, the means used to teach a skill are as important as the skill itself.   7.____
In teaching adults, which of the following would be MOST appropriate?

    A. Working individually with someone after dinner in order to teach him or her how to brush their teeth

    B. Teaching pouring skills with sand in a sandbox

    C. Teaching how to button clothes by using a doll for practice

    D. Teaching how to tie shoelaces by first working With a baby shoe

8. Which of the following statements is TRUE?   8.____

    A. Residents' chore duties in a community residence should only change three times a year.

    B. Entrance into a community residence should be solely determined by an individual's need for a place to live.

    C. Using a task analysis for a client would involve breaking down a complex task into smaller, more understandable parts.

    D. Clients should be allowed to eat when and what they choose.

9. Select the one statement below that is NOT true of supervised community residences.   9.____
A supervised community residence

    A. can provide short-term residence for individuals who need only training and experience in activities of daily living after a period of institutionalization or as an alternative to institutionalization

    B. can provide an institutional setting for those people who need it

    C. can provide long-term residence for individuals who are unlikely to acquire the skills necessary for more independent living

    D. usually requires staff on site at all times

10. All of the following are goals of community residences EXCEPT   10.____

    A. providing a home environment for developmentally disabled persons

    B. providing a setting where clients can learn the skills necessary to live in the least restrictive environment

    C. providing a setting where the developmentally disabled can acquire the skills necessary to live as independently as possible

    D. the community residence allows for the maximum level of independence inconsistent with a person's disability and functional level

11. All of the following statements are true EXCEPT: 11.____

    A. A community residence does not need to adhere to the principle of normalization in its physical or social structure

    B. The term least restrictive environment refers to an environment which most resembles that of non-handicapped peers where the needs of developmentally disabled persons can be met

C. A person's length of stay in a community residence extends only until a person has attained the skills and motivation to function successfully in a less restrictive setting

D. The purposes of a community residence may vary so that people with different ranges of abilities and levels of functioning may be served

12. All of the following statements are true EXCEPT: 12._____

    A. Developmentally disabled persons residing in community residences must be afforded privacy, personal space, and freedom of access to the house as is consistent with their age and program needs

    B. Transportation should be available from the nearest institution so that people in community residences have access to the community

    C. The service needs of each person in a community residence should be individually planned by an interdisciplinary team

    D. An interdisciplinary team should include staff of the community residence, providers of program and support services, and, if appropriate, the developmentally disabled person's correspondent

13. All of the following statements are true EXCEPT: 13._____

    A. Supportive community residences are not required to provide staff on site 24 hours a day

    B. Residents in supervised community residences may need more assistance in activities of daily living than persons residing in supportive community residences

    C. An aim of a community residence is to maintain a family and home-like environment

    D. Those living in a community residence shall spend at least three hours per weekday and one evening per week in programs and activities at the residence

14. In working in treatment teams, it is MOST important for team members to   14._____

    A. communicate effectively with each other
    B. keep morale high
    C. attend meetings on time
    D. enjoy working with each other

15. All of the following statements are true EXCEPT: 15._____

    A. In teaching self-care skills, many tasks may need to be divided into sub-parts
    B. Tasks which are easiest to learn should generally be taught first
    C. Changes in routine are very helpful when teaching the mentally retarded a new skill
    D. The severely retarded do not learn as well from verbal instruction as they do from demonstration of a skill

16. All of the following statements are true EXCEPT: 16._____

    A. It is important to evaluate the client's readiness to attempt learning a particular task before starting to teach the task

    B. It is better to do a task for a client if the task may take much time and effort on his or her part

    C. People generally learn faster when their efforts lead to an enjoyable activity

    D. It is best when teaching a certain skill to begin with a small group when possible

17. All of the following statements are true EXCEPT: 17._____

    A. The expectations of a staff person of how well a client will be able to perform a certain task can influence daily living skills
    B. Environmental factors can influence daily living skills
    C. After seeing a skill demonstrated, a client should practice the skill
    D. A client will make a greater effort if he or she feels ill at ease with the instructor, and knows the instructor will become impatient if he or she continues to make mistakes

18. Of the following, the BEST way to teach a client an activity of daily living is to   18._____

    A. describe the steps to the client
    B. read the directions to the client
    C. break the activity into steps and have the client learn one step at a time
    D. have a client who can perform the task teach the client who cannot

19. All of the following are important steps in teaching a living skill EXCEPT   19._____

    A. defining the skill clearly
    B. determining the size of the skill
    C. breaking down each major step into substeps and sub-substeps as necessary
    D. rewarding the accomplishment of each step with candy

20. When teaching a daily living skill, it is important to keep in mind all of the following EXCEPT   20._____

    A. using concrete and specific language
    B. punishment can be a highly effective learning device
    C. matching the size of the skill to the client's ability level
    D. demonstrating what you want the resident to do

KEY (CORRECT ANSWERS)

1.	C		11.	A
2.	D		12.	B
3.	B		13.	D
4.	A		14.	A
5.	D		15.	C
6.	C		16.	B
7.	A		17.	D
8.	C		18.	C
9.	B		19.	D
10.	D		20.	B

TEST 2

Each question or incomplete statement is followed by several suggested answers or completions. Select the one that BEST answers the question or completes the statement. *PRINT THE LETTER OF THE CORRECT ANSWER IN THE SPACE AT THE RIGHT.*

1. All of the following would be considered qualities of a developmental disability EXCEPT the disability

   A. may be attributable to mental retardation or autism
   B. has continued or can be expected to continue indefinitely
   C. can be easily overcome
   D. may be attributable to cerebral palsy or neurological impairment

   1._____

2. The condition of autism

   A. applies to those people who have little or no control over their motor skills
   B. is hereditary
   C. is characterized by severe disorders of communication and behavior
   D. begins most frequently in adulthood

   2._____

3. Secondary childhood autism differs from primary childhood autism in that

   A. primary childhood autism is more difficult to treat
   B. secondary childhood autism is secondary to disturbances such as brain damage
   C. secondary childhood autism is not as severe a disorder
   D. secondary childhood autism is less likely to interfere with behavior patterns

   3._____

4. Which of the following would be LEAST adversely affected by autism?

   A. Interpersonal relations
   B. Learning
   C. Developmental rate and sequences
   D. Motor skills

   4._____

5. Which of the following statements is NOT true?

   A. Cerebral palsy refers to a condition resulting from damage to the brain that may occur before, during or after birth and results in the loss of control over voluntary muscles in the body.
   B. Ataxic cerebral palsy is characterized by an inability to maintain normal balance.
   C. Someone with athetoid cerebral palsy would find it easier to maintain purposeful-ness of movements than someone with spastic cerebral palsy.
   D. Mixed cerebral palsy refers to the combination of two or more of the following categories of cerebral palsy such as the spastic, athetoid, ataxic, tremor, and rigid types.

   5._____

6. All of the following are true about epilepsy EXCEPT

   A. epilepsy does not usually involve a loss of consciousness
   B. an *aura* often appears to the individual before a *grand mal* seizure occurs

   6._____

    C.   people experiencing *petit mal* seizures are seldom aware that a seizure has occurred

    D.   status epilepticus, psychomotor, and Jacksonian are all forms of epilepsy

7.   All of the following statements are true of mental retardation EXCEPT: 7._____

    A.   The prevalence of mental retardation in the general total population is less than 3% of the population

    B.   Approximately 89% of the mentally retarded population is mildly retarded

    C.   School-age children who are mildly retarded can usually acquire practical skills and useful reading and arithmetic skills

    D.   Adults who are mildly retarded can not usually achieve social and vocational skills adequate for minimum self-support

8.   Which of the following statements is NOT true of mental retardation?   8._____

    A.   Approximately 6% of the mentally retarded population is moderately retarded (I.Q. 36-51), 3.5% of the mentally retarded population is severely retarded (I.Q. 20-35), and 1.5% of this population is profoundly retarded (I.Q. 19 and below).

    B.   A profoundly retarded person could never achieve limited self-care.

    C.   Moderately retarded adults may achieve self-maintenance in unskilled work or semi-skilled work under sheltered conditions.

    D.   Severely retarded children can profit from systematic skills training.

9.   All of the following refer to neurological impairment EXCEPT   9._____

    A.   childhood aphasia is a condition characterized by the failure to develop, or difficulty in using, language and speech

    B.   epilepsy

    C.   minimal brain dysfunction is associated with deviations of the central nervous system

    D.   neurological impairment refers to a group of disorders of the central nervous system characterized by dysfunction in one or more, but not all, skills affecting communicative, perceptual, cognitive, memory, attentional, motor control, and appropriate social behaviors

10.   Which of the following statements is TRUE?   10._____

    A.   Autistic children are below average in intelligence level.

    B.   All cerebral palsied persons are mentally retarded.

    C.   Once an epileptic seizure has started, it cannot be stopped.

    D.   Autism is due to faulty early interactional patterns between child and mother.

11.   All of the following are false EXCEPT   11._____

    A.   recent investigations have found that parents of autistic children have no specific common personality traits and no unusual environmental stresses

    B.   cerebral palsied persons cannot understand directions

    C.   it is not true that unless controlled seizures can cause further brain damage

    D.   the majority of the mentally retarded are in institutions

12. In serving the needs of autistic persons, the one of the following which is usually LEAST important is the need

    A. for training in social skills
    B. for language stimulation
    C. to deal with potentially self-injurious, repetitive, and aggressive behaviors
    D. to teach skills that would improve intelligence

12.____

13. In serving the needs of persons with cerebral palsy, the one of the following which is usually LEAST important is the need

    A. to experience normal movement and sensations as much as possible
    B. to develop fundamental movement patterns which the person can regulate
    C. for experience and guidance in social settings
    D. to restrict their environment

13.____

14. All of the following statements are true EXCEPT:

    A. It is important that epileptic persons have balanced diets
    B. Pica, a craving for unnatural food, occurs with all mentally retarded persons
    C. It has been projected that 50% of those individuals who have cerebral palsy are also mentally retarded
    D. When working with the mentally retarded, it is important to encourage sensory-motor stimulation, physical stimulation, language stimulation, social skills training, and the performance of daily living skills

14.____

15. When working with neurologically impaired persons, all of the following are true EXCEPT:

    A. There is usually a need for perceptual training
    B. It is important to keep in mind that an individual may know something one day and not know it the next
    C. It may be necessary to remove distracting stimuli
    D. It is important to keep in mind that neurologically impaired persons usually have substantially lower I.Q.'s than the average person

15.____

16. The developmentally disabled do NOT have the right to

    A. register and vote in elections
    B. marry
    C. confidentiality of records
    D. hit someone who teases them

16.____

17. Which of the following statements is TRUE?

    A. It is important for staff members not to make all of the choices for their mentally retarded clients.
    B. Distraction is not a good technique to use when trying to channel potentially violent or destructive behavior to a socially acceptable outlet.
    C. Severely and profoundly retarded children do not appear to have a strong need for personal contact.
    D. It is primarily the mildly or moderately retarded child that exhibits the behavior usually associated with mental retardation.

17.____

18. All of the following are causes of mental retardation EXCEPT

    A. organic defects
    B. brain lesions
    C. increased sexual activity
    D. chromosomal abnormalities

18.____

19. A mentally retarded patient who is *acting out*

    A. may be trying to communicate that he or she is physically uncomfortable or needs something
    B. should be ignored
    C. should be severely punished
    D. feels comfortable in his or her surroundings

19.____

20. In working with the developmentally disabled, all of the following would be appropriate EXCEPT

    A. remembering that seemingly small things, both positive and negative, can be very important to the client
    B. allowing choices whenever possible
    C. maintaining a calm, level-headed attitude during an anxiety-producing situation will reassure clients and help them relax and feel safer
    D. after basic self-help skills have been mastered, it is not necessary to encourage further development

20.____

KEY (CORRECT ANSWERS)

1.	C		11.	A
2.	C		12.	D
3.	B		13.	D
4.	D		14.	B
5.	C		15.	D
6.	A		16.	D
7.	D		17.	A
8.	B		18.	C
9.	B		19.	A
10.	C		20.	D

EXAMINATION SECTION
TEST 1

DIRECTIONS: Each question or incomplete statement is followed by several suggested answers or completions. Select the one that BEST answers the question or completes the statement. *PRINT THE LETTER OF THE CORRECT ANSWER IN THE SPACE AT THE RIGHT.*

Questions 1-10.

DIRECTIONS: For each of the sentences given below, numbered 1 through 10, select from the following choices the MOST correct choice and print your choice in the space at the right. Select as your answer:
- A – if the statement contains an unnecessary word of expression
- B – if the statement contains a slang term or expression ordinarily not acceptable in government report writing
- C – if the statement contains an old-fashioned word or expression, where a concrete, plain term would be more useful
- D – if the statement contains no major faults

1. Every one of us should try harder.   1._____

2. Yours of the first instant has been received.   2._____

3. We will have to do a real snow job on him.   3._____

4. I shall contact him next Thursday.   4._____

5. None of us were invited to the meeting with the community.   5._____

6. We got this here job to do.   6._____

7. She could not help but see the mistake in the checkbook.   7._____

8. Don't bug the Director about the report.   8._____

9. I beg to inform you that your letter has been received.   9._____

10. This project is all screwed up.   10._____

Questions 11-15.

DIRECTIONS: Read the following Inter-office Memo. Then answer Questions 11 through 15 based ONLY on the memo.

INTER-OFFICE MEMORANDUM

To: Alma Robinson, Human Resources Aide
From: Frank Shields, Social Worker

I would like to have you help Mr. Edward Tunney who is trying to raise his two children by himself. He needs to learn to improve the physical care of his children and especially of his daughter Helen, age 9. She is avoided and ridiculed at school because her hair is uncombed, her teeth not properly cleaned, her clothing torn, wrinkled and dirty, as well as shabby and poorly fitted. The teachers and school officials have contacted the Department and the social worker for two years about Helen. She is not able to make friends because of these problems. I have talked to Mr. Tunney about improvements for the child's clothing, hair, and hygiene. He tends to deny these things are problems, but is cooperative, and a second person showing him the importance of better physical care for Helen would be helpful.

Perhaps you could teach Helen how to fix her own hair. She has all the materials. I would also like you to form your own opinion of the sanitary conditions in the home and how they could be improved.

Mr. Tunney is expecting your visit and is willing to talk with you about ways he can help with these problems.

11. In the above memorandum, the Human Resources Aide is being asked to help Mr. Tunney to   11.____

    A.   improve the learning habits of his children
    B.   enable his children to make friends at school
    C.   take responsibility for the upbringing of his children
    D.   give attention to the grooming and cleanliness of his children

12. This case was brought to the attention of the social worker by   12.____

    A.   government officials
    B.   teachers and school officials
    C.   the Department
    D.   Mr. Tunney

13. In general, Mr. Tunney's attitude with regard to his children could BEST be described as   13.____

    A.   interested in correcting the obvious problems, but unable to do so alone
    B.   unwilling to follow the advice of those who are trying to help
    C.   concerned, but unaware of the seriousness of these problems
    D.   interested in helping them, but afraid of taking the advice of the social worker

14. Which of the following actions has NOT been suggested as a possible step for the Human Resources Aide to take?   14.____

    A.   Help Helen to learn to care for herself by teaching her grooming skills
    B.   Determine ways of improvement through information gathered on a home visit
    C.   Discuss her own views on Helen's problems with school officials
    D.   Ask Mr. Tunney in what ways he believes the physical care may be improved

15. According to the memo, the Human Resources Aide is ESPECIALLY being asked to observe and form her own opinions about

    A. the relationship between Mr. Tunney and the school officials
    B. Helen's attitude toward her classmates and teacher
    C. the sanitary conditions in the home
    D. the reasons Mr. Tunney is not cooperative with the agency

15.____

16. In one day, an aide receives 18 inquiries by phone and 27 inquiries in person. What percentage of the inquiries received that day were by phone?

    A. 33%   B. 40%   C. 45%   D. 60%

16.____

17. If the weekly pay checks for 5 part-time employees are: $129.32, $162.74, $143.67, $135.75, and $156.56, then the combined weekly income for the 5 employees is

    A. $727.84   B. $728.04   C. $730.84   D. $737.04

17.____

18. Suppose that there are 17 aides working in an office where many community complaints are received by telephone. In one ten-day period, 4250 calls were received. If the same number of calls were received each day, and the aides divided the work load equally, about how many calls did each aide respond to daily?

    A. 25   B. 35   C. 75   D. 250

18.____

19. Suppose that an assignment was divided among 5 aides. If the first aide spent 67 hours on the assignment, the second aide spent 95 hours, the third aide spent 52 hours, the fourth aide spent 78 hours, and the fifth aide spent 103 hours, what was the AVERAGE amount of time spent by each aide on the assignment?
_____ hours.

    A. 71   B. 75   C. 79   D. 83

19.____

20. If there are 240 employees in a center and 1/3 are absent on the day of a bad snow-storm, how many employees were at work in the center on that day?

    A. 80   B. 120   C. 160   D. 200

20.____

KEY (CORRECT ANSWERS)

1.	D	11.	D
2.	C	12.	B
3.	B	13.	C
4.	D	14.	C
5.	D	15.	C
6.	B	16.	B
7.	D	17.	B
8.	B	18.	A
9.	C	19.	C
10.	B	20.	C

TEST 2

DIRECTIONS: Each question or incomplete statement is followed by several suggested answers or completions. Select the one that BEST answers the question or completes the statement. *PRINT THE LETTER OF THE CORRECT ANSWER IN THE SPACE AT THE RIGHT.*

1. Suppose that an aide takes 25 minutes to prepare a letter to a client.
   If the aide is assigned to prepare 9 letters on a certain day, how much time should she set aside for this task? _____ hours.   1.____

   A. 3 3/4   B. 4 1/4   C. 4 3/4   D. 5 1/4

2. Suppose that a certain center uses both Form A and Form B in the course of its daily work, and that Form A is used 4 times as often as Form B.
   If the total number of both forms used in one week is 750, how many times was Form A used?   2.____

   A. 100   B. 200   C. 400   D. 600

3. Suppose a center has a budget of $1092.70 from which 8 desks costing $78.05 apiece must be bought?
   How many ADDITIONAL desks can be ordered from this budget after the 8 desks have been purchased?   3.____

   A. 4   B. 6   C. 9   D. 14

4. When researching a particular case, a team of 16 aides was asked to check through 234 folders to obtain the necessary information.
   If half the aides worked twice as fast as the other half, and the slow group checked through 12 folders each hour, about how long would it take to complete the assignment? _____ hours.   4.____

   A. $4\frac{1}{4}$ B. 5   C. 6   D. $6\frac{1}{2}$

5. The difference in the cost of two printers is $28.32. If the less expensive printer costs $153.61, what is the cost of the other printer?   5.____

   A. $171.93   B. $172.03   C. $181.93   D. $182.03

Questions 6-8.

DIRECTIONS: Questions 6 through 8 are to be answered on the basis of the following information contained on a sample page of a payroll book.

Emp. No.	Name of Employee	\multicolumn{5}{c}{Hours Worked}					Total Hours Worked	Pay PerHour	Total Wages
		M	T	W	Th	F			
1	James Smith	8	8	8	8	8			$480.00
2	Gloria Jones	8	7 3/4	7	7 1/2			$16.00	$560.00
3	Robert Adams	6	6	71/2	71/2	8 3/4		$18.28	

52

6. The pay per hour of Employee No. 1 is   6.____

   A. $12.00   B. $13.72   C. $15.00   D. $19.20

7. The number of hours that Employee No. 2 worked on Friday is   7.____

   A. 4   B. 5 1/2   C. 4.63   D. 4 3/4

8. The total wages for Employee No. 3 is   8.____

   A. $636.92   B. $648.94   C. $661.04   D. $672.96

9. As a rule, the FIRST step in writing a check should be to   9.____

   A. number the check
   B. write in the payee's name
   C. tear out the check stub
   D. write the purpose of the check in the space provided at the bottom

10. If an error is made when writing a check, the MOST widely accepted procedure is to   10.____

   A. draw a line through the error and initial it
   B. destroy both the check and check stub by tearing into small pieces
   C. erase the error if it does not occur in the amount of the check
   D. write *Void* across both the check and check stub and save them

11. The check that is MOST easily cashed is one that is   11.____

   A. not signed   B. made payable to *Cash*
   C. post-dated   D. endorsed in part

12.   12.____

No. *103*	$ *142. 77*
May 14	
To *Alan Jacobs*	
For *Wages (5/6-5/10)*	
Bal. Bro't For'd	2340. 63
Amt. Deposited	205. 24
Total	
Amt. This Check	142. 77
Bal. Car'd For'd	

The balance to be carried forward on the check stub above is
   A. $2,278.16   B. $1,992.62   C. $2,688.64   D. $2,403.10

13. The procedure for reconciling a bank statement consists of _____ the bank balance   13.____
and _____ the checkbook balance.

   A. *adding* outstanding checks to; *subtracting* the service and check charges from
   B. *subtracting* the service charge from; *subtracting* outstanding checks from
   C. *subtracting* the service charge from; *adding* outstanding checks to
   D. *subtracting* outstanding checks from; *subtracting* the service and check charges from

14. An employee makes $15.70 an hour and receives time-and-a-half in overtime pay for every hour more than 40 in a given week. If the employee works 47 hours, the employee's total wages for that week would be 14.____

    A. $792.85   B. $837.90   C. $875.25   D. $1,106.85

15. A high-speed copier can make 25,000 copies before periodic service is required. Before this service is necessary, _____ copies of a 137-page document can be printed. 15.____

    A. 211   B. 204   C. 190   D. 178

16. An aide is typing a letter to the James Weldon Johnson Head Start Center. To be sure that a Mr. Joseph Maxwell reads it, an attention line is typed below the inside address. The salutation should, therefore, read: 16.____

    A. To Whom It May Concern: B. Dear Mr. Maxwell:
    C. Gentlemen: D. Dear Joseph:

17. When describing the advantages of the numeric filing system, it is NOT true that it 17.____

    A. is the most accurate of all methods
    B. allows for unlimited expansion according to the needs of the agency
    C. is a system useful for filing letters directly according to name or subject
    D. allows for cross-referencing

18. In writing a letter for your Center, the PURPOSE of the letter should usually be stated in 18.____

    A. the first paragraph. This assists the reader in making more sense of the letter.
    B. the second paragraph. The first paragraph should be used to confirm receipt of the letter being answered
    C. the last paragraph. The first paragraphs should be used to build up to the purpose of the letter.
    D. any paragraph. Each letter has a different purpose and the letter should conform to that purpose.

19. If you open a personal letter addressed to another aide by mistake, the one of the following actions which it would generally be BEST for you to take is to 19.____

    A. reseal the envelope or place the contents in another envelope and pass it on to the employee
    B. place the letter inside the envelope, indicate under your initials that it was opened in error and give it to the employee
    C. personally give the employee the letter without any explanation
    D. ignore your error, attach the envelope to the letter, and give it out in the usual manner

20. Of the following, the MAIN purpose of the head start program is to 20.____

    A. provide programs for pre-school development of children
    B. provide children between the ages of 6 and 12 with after-school activity
    C. establish a system for providing care for teenage youngsters with working parents
    D. supervise centers providing 24-hour child care

KEY (CORRECT ANSWERS)

1.	A		11.	B
2.	D		12.	D
3.	B		13.	D
4.	D		14.	A
5.	C		15.	D
6.	A		16.	C
7.	D		17.	C
8.	B		18.	A
9.	A		19.	B
10.	D		20.	A

———

READING COMPREHENSION
UNDERSTANDING AND INTERPRETING WRITTEN MATERIAL
EXAMINATION SECTION
TEST 1

Questions 1-8.

DIRECTIONS: Each question or incomplete statement is followed by several suggested answers or completions. Select the one that BEST answers the question or completes the statement. *PRINT THE LETTER OF THE CORRECT ANSWER IN THE SPACE AT THE RIGHT.*

Questions 1 and 2.

DIRECTIONS: Your answers to Questions 1 and 2 must be based ONLY on the information given in the following paragraph.

Hospitals maintained wholly by public taxation may treat only those compensation cases which are emergencies and may not treat such emergency cases longer than the emergency exists; provided, however, that these restrictions shall not be applicable where there is not available a hospital other than a hospital maintained wholly by taxation.

1. According to the above paragraph, compensation cases   1.____

    A. are regarded as emergency cases by hospitals maintained wholly by public taxation
    B. are seldom treated by hospitals maintained wholly by public taxation
    C. are treated mainly by privately endowed hospitals
    D. may be treated by hospitals maintained wholly by public taxation if they are emergencies

2. According to the above paragraph, it is MOST reasonable to conclude that where a privately endowed hospital is available,   2.____

    A. a hospital supported wholly by public taxation may treat emergency compensation cases only so long as the emergency exists
    B. a hospital supported wholly by public taxation may treat any compensation cases
    C. a hospital supported wholly by public taxation must refer emergency compensation cases to such a hospital
    D. the restrictions regarding the treatment of compensation cases by a tax-supported hospital are not wholly applicable

Questions 3-7.

DIRECTIONS: Answer Questions 3 through 7 ONLY according to the information given in the following passage.

THE MANUFACTURE OF LAUNDRY SOAP

The manufacture of soap is not a complicated process. Soap is a fat or an oil, plus an alkali, water and salt. The alkali used in making commercial laundry soap is caustic soda. The salt used is the same as common table salt. A fat is generally an animal product that is not a liquid at room temperature. If heated, it becomes a liquid. An oil is generally liquid at room temperature. If the temperature is lowered, the oil becomes a solid just like ordinary fat.

At the soap plant, a huge tank five stories high, called a *kettle,* is first filled part way with fats and then the alkali and water are added. These ingredients are then heated and boiled together. Salt is then poured into the top of the boiling solution; and as the salt slowly sinks down through the mixture, it takes with it the glycerine which comes from the melted fats. The product which finally comes from the kettle is a clear soap which has a moisture content of about 34%. This clear soap is then chilled so that more moisture is driven out. As a result, the manufacturer finally ends up with a commercial laundry soap consisting of 88% clear soap and only 12% moisture.

3.   An ingredient used in making laundry soap is

    A.   table sugar   B.   potash
    C.   glycerine   D.   caustic soda

3.___

4.   According to the above passage, a difference between fats and oils is that fats

    A.   cost more than oils
    B.   are solid at room temperature
    C.   have less water than oils
    D.   are a liquid animal product

4.___

5.   According to the above passage, the MAIN reason for using salt in the manufacture of soap is to

    A.   make the ingredients boil together
    B.   keep the fats in the kettle melted
    C.   remove the glycerine
    D.   prevent the loss of water from the soap

5.___

6.   According to the passage, the purpose of chilling the clear soap is to

    A.   stop the glycerine from melting
    B.   separate the alkali from the fats
    C.   make the oil become solid
    D.   get rid of more moisture

6.___

7.   According to the passage, the percentage of moisture in commercial laundry soap is

    A.   12%   B.   34%   C.   66%   D.   88%

7.___

8. The x-ray has gone into business. Developed primarily to aid in diagnosing human ills, the machine now works in packing plants, in foundries, in service stations, and in a dozen ways to contribute to precision and accuracy in industry.
The above statement means *most nearly* that the x-ray

    A. was first developed to aid business
    B. is of more help to business than it is to medicine
    C. is being used to improve the functioning of business
    D. is more accurate for packing plants than it is for foundries

8.____

Questions 9-25.

DIRECTIONS: Each question consists of a statement. You are to indicate whether the statement is TRUE (T) or FALSE (F). *PRINT THE LETTER OF THE CORRECT ANSWER IN THE SPACE AT THE RIGHT.*

Questions 9-12.

DIRECTIONS: Read the paragraph below about *shock* and then answer Questions 9 through 12 according to the information given in the paragraph.

<u>SHOCK</u>

While not found in all injuries, shock is present in all serious injuries caused by accidents. During shock, the normal activities of the body slow down. This partly explains why one of the signs of shock is a pale, cold skin, since insufficient blood goes to the body parts during shock.

9.   If the injury caused by an accident is serious, shock is sure to be present.

9.____

10. In shock, the heart beats faster than normal.

10.____

11. The face of a person suffering from shock is usually red and flushed.

11.____

12. Not enough blood goes to different parts of the body during shock.

12.____

Questions 13-18.

DIRECTIONS: Questions 13 through 18, inclusive, are to be answered SOLELY on the basis of the information contained in the following statement and NOT upon any other information you may have.

Blood transfusions are given to patients at the hospital upon recommendation of the physicians attending such cases. The physician fills out a *Request for Blood Transfusion* form in duplicate and sends both copies to the Medical Director's office, where a list is maintained of persons called *donors* who desire to sell their blood for transfusions. A suitable donor is selected, and the transfusion is given. Donors are, in many instances, medical students and employees of the hospital. Donors receive twenty-five dollars for each transfusion.

13. According to the above paragraph, a blood donor is paid twenty-five dollars for each transfusion.

13.____

14. According to the above paragraph, only medical students and employees of the hospital are selected as blood donors.   14.___

15. According to the above paragraph, the *Request for Blood Transfusion* form is filled out by the patient and sent to the Medical Director's office.   15.___

16. According to the above paragraph, a list of blood donors is maintained in the Medical Director's office.   16.___

17. According to the above paragraph, cases for which the attending physicians recommend blood transfusions are usually emergency cases.   17.___

18. According to the above paragraph, one copy of the *Request for Blood Transfusion* form is kept by the patient and one copy is sent to the Medical Director's office.   18.___

Questions 19-25.

DIRECTIONS: Questions 19 through 25, inclusive, are to be answered SOLELY on the basis of the information contained in the following passage and NOT upon any other information you may have.

Before being admitted to a hospital ward, a patient is first interviewed by the Admitting Clerk, who records the patient's name, age, sex, race, birthplace, and mother's maiden name. This clerk takes all of the money and valuables that the patient has on his person. A list of the valuables is written on the back of the envelope in which the valuables are afterwards placed. Cash is counted and placed in a separate envelope, and the amount of money and the name of the patient are written on the outside of the envelope. Both envelopes are sealed, fastened together, and placed in a compartment of a safe.

An orderly then escorts the patient to a dressing room where the patient's clothes are removed and placed in a bundle. A tag bearing the patient's name is fastened to the bundle. A list of the contents of the bundle is written on property slips, which are made out in triplicate. The information contained on the outside of the envelopes containing the cash and valuables belonging to the patient is also copied on the property slips.

According to the above passage,

19. patients are escorted to the dressing room by the Admitting Clerk.   19.___

20. the patient's cash and valuables are placed together in one envelope.   20.___

21. the number of identical property slips that are made out when a patient is being admitted to a hospital ward is three.   21.___

22. the full names of both parents of a patient are recorded by the Admitting Clerk before a patient is admitted to a hospital ward.   22.___

23. the amount of money that a patient has on his person when admitted to the hospital is entered on the patient's property slips.   23.___

24. an orderly takes all the money and valuables that a patient has on his person.   24.___

25. the patient's name is placed on the tag that is attached to the bundle containing the patient's clothing.   25.___

KEY (CORRECT ANSWERS)

1.	D	11.	F
2.	A	12.	T
3.	D	13.	T
4.	B	14.	F
5.	C	15.	F
6.	D	16.	T
7.	A	17.	T
8.	C	18.	F
9.	T	19.	F
10.	F	20.	F

21.	T
22.	F
23.	T
24.	F
25.	T

TEST 2

Questions 1-4.

DIRECTIONS: Questions 1 through 4 are to be answered in accordance with the following paragraphs.

One fundamental difference between the United States health care system and the health care systems of some European countries is the way that hospital charges for long-term illnesses affect their citizens.

In European countries such as England, Sweden, and Germany, citizens can face, without fear, hospital charges due to prolonged illness, no matter how substantial they may be. Citizens of these nations are required to pay nothing when they are hospitalized, for they have prepaid their treatment as taxpayers when they were well and were earning incomes.

On the other hand, the United States citizen, in spite of the growth of payments by third parties which include private insurance carriers as well as public resources, has still to shoulder 40 percent of hospital care costs, while his private insurance contributes only 25 percent and public resources the remaining 35 percent.

Despite expansion of private health insurance and social legislation in the United States, out-of-pocket payments for hospital care by individuals have steadily increased. Such payments, currently totalling $23 billion, are nearly twice as high as ten years ago.

Reform is inevitable and, when it comes, will have to reconcile sharply conflicting interests. Hospital staffs are demanding higher and higher wages. Hospitals are under pressure by citizens, who as patients demand more and better services but who as taxpayers or as subscribers to hospital insurance plans, are reluctant to pay the higher cost of improved care. An acceptable reconciliation of these interests has so far eluded legislators and health administrators in the United States.

1.   According to the above passage, the one of the following which is an ADVANTAGE that citizens of England, Sweden, and Germany have over United States citizens is that, when faced with long-term illness,   1.___

   A.   the amount of out-of-pocket payments made by these European citizens is small when compared to out-of-pocket payments made by United States citizens
   B.   European citizens have no fear of hospital costs no matter how great they may be
   C.   more efficient and reliable hospitals are available to the European citizen than is available to the United States citizens
   D.   a greater range of specialized hospital care is available to the European citizens than is available to the United States citizens

2. According to the above passage, reform of the United States system of health care must reconcile all of the following EXCEPT   2.____

    A. attempts by health administrators to provide improved hospital care
    B. taxpayers' reluctance to pay for the cost of more and better hospital services
    C. demands by hospital personnel for higher wages
    D. insurance subscribers' reluctance to pay the higher costs of improved hospital care

3. According to the above passage, the out-of-pocket payments for hospital care that individuals made ten years ago was APPROXIMATELY _____ billion.   3.____

    A. $32   B. $23   C. $12   D. $3

4. According to the above passage, the GREATEST share of the costs of hospital care in the United States is paid by   4.____

    A. United States citizens   B. private insurance carriers
    C. public resources   D. third parties

Questions 5-8.

DIRECTIONS: Questions 5 through 8 are to be answered SOLELY on the basis of the information contained in the following passage.

Effective cost controls have been difficult to establish in most hospitals in the United States. Ways must be found to operate hospitals with reasonable efficiency without sacrificing quality and in a manner that will reduce the amount of personal income now being spent on health care and the enormous drain on national resources. We must adopt a new public objective of providing higher quality health care at significantly lower cost. One step that can be taken to achieve this goal is to carefully control capital expenditures for hospital construction and expansion. Perhaps the way to start is to declare a moratorium on all hospital construction and to determine the factors that should be considered in deciding whether a hospital should be built. Such factors might include population growth, distance to the nearest hospital, availability of medical personnel, and hospital bed shortage.

A second step to achieve the new objective is to increase the ratio of out-of-hospital patient to in-hospital patient care. This can be done by using separate health care facilities other than hospitals to attract patients who have increasingly been going to hospital clinics and overcrowding them. Patients should instead identify with a separate health care facility to keep them out of hospitals.

A third step is to require better hospital operating rules and controls. This step might include the review of a doctor's performance by other doctors, outside professional evaluations of medical practice, and required refresher courses and re-examinations for doctors. Other measures might include obtaining mandatory second opinions on the need for surgery in order to avoid unnecessary surgery, and outside review of work rules and procedures to eliminate unnecessary testing of patients.

A fourth step is to halt the construction and public subsidizing of new medical schools and to fill whatever needs exist in professional coverage by emphasizing the medical training of physicians with specialities that are in short supply and by providing a better geographic distribution of physicians and surgeons.

5. According to the above passage, providing higher quality health care at lower cost can be achieved by the   5.___

    A. greater use of out-of-hospital facilities
    B. application of more effective cost controls on doctors' fees
    C. expansion of improved in-hospital patient care services at hospital clinics
    D. development of more effective training programs in hospital administration

6. According to the above passage, the one of the following which should be taken into account in determining if a hospital should be constructed is the   6.___

    A. number of out-of-hospital health care facilities
    B. availability of public funds to subsidize construction
    C. number of hospitals under construction
    D. availability of medical personnel

7. According to the above passage, it is IMPORTANT to operate hospitals efficiently because   7.___

    A. they are currently in serious financial difficulties
    B. of the need to reduce the amount of personal income going to health care
    C. the quality of health care services has deteriorated
    D. of the need to increase productivity goals to take care of the growing population in the United States

8. According to the above passage, which one of the following approaches is MOST LIKELY to result in better operating rules and controls in hospitals?   8.___

    A. Allocating doctors to health care facilities on the basis of patient population
    B. Equalizing the workloads of doctors
    C. Establishing a physician review board to evaluate the performance of other physicians
    D. Eliminating unnecessary outside review of patient testing

Questions 9-14.

DIRECTIONS: Questions 9 through 14 are to be answered SOLELY on the basis of the information contained in the following passage.

The United States today is the only major industrial nation in the world without a system of national health insurance or a national health service. Instead, we have placed our prime reliance on private enterprise and private health insurance to meet the need. Yet, in a recent year, of the 180 million Americans under 65 years of age, 34 million had no hospital insurance, 38 million had no surgical insurance, 63 million had no out-patient x-ray and laboratory insurance, 94 million had no insurance for prescription drugs, and 103 million had no insurance for physician office visits or home visits. Some 35 million Americans under the age of 65 had no health insurance whatsoever. Some 64 million additional Americans under age 65 had health insurance coverage that was less than that provided to the aged under Medicare.

Despite more than three decades of enormous growth, the private health insurance industry today pays benefits equal to only one-third of the total cost of private health care, leaving the rest to be borne by the patient—essentially the same ratio which held true a decade ago. Moreover, nearly all private health insurance is limited; it provides partial benefits, not comprehensive benefits; acute care, not preventive care; it siphons off the young and healthy, and ignores the poor and medically indigent. The typical private carrier usually pays only the cost of hospital care, forcing physicians and patients alike to resort to wasteful and inefficient use of hospital facilities, thereby giving further impetus to the already soaring costs of hospital care. Valuable hospital beds are used for routine tests and examinations. Unnecessary hospitalization, unnecessary surgery, and unnecessarily extended hospital stays are encouraged. These problems are exacerbated by the fact that administrative costs of commercial carriers are substantially higher than they are for Blue Shield, Blue Cross, or Medicare.

9. According to the above passage, the PROPORTION of total private health care costs paid by private health insurance companies today as compared to ten years ago has   9._____

    A. *increased* by approximately one-third
    B. *remained* practically the same
    C. *increased* by approximately two-thirds
    D. *decreased* by approximately one-third

10. According to the above passage, the one of the following which has contributed MOST to wasteful use of hospital facilities is the   10._____

    A. increased emphasis on preventive health care
    B. practice of private carriers of providing comprehensive health care benefits
    C. increased hospitalization of the elderly and the poor
    D. practice of a number of private carriers of paying only for hospital care costs

11. Based on the information in the above passage, which one of the following patients would be LEAST likely to receive benefits from a typical private health insurance plan? A   11._____

    A. young patient who must undergo an emergency appendectomy
    B. middle-aged patient who needs a costly series of x-ray and laboratory tests for diagnosis of gastrointestinal complaints
    C. young patient who must visit his physician weekly for treatment of a chronic skin disease
    D. middle-aged patient who requires extensive cancer surgery

12. Which one of the following is the MOST accurate inference that can be drawn from the above passage?   12._____

    A. Private health insurance has failed to fully meet the health care needs of Americans.
    B. Most Americans under age 65 have health insurance coverage better than that provided to the elderly under Medicare.
    C. Countries with a national health service are likely to provide poorer health care for their citizens than do countries that rely primarily on private health insurance.
    D. Hospital facilities in the United States are inadequate to meet the nation's health care needs.

13. Of the total number of Americans under age 65, what percentage belonged in the combined category of persons with NO health insurance or health insurance less than that provided to the aged under Medicare?

    A. 19%   B. 36%   C. 55%   D. 65%

13._____

14. According to the above passage, the one of the following types of health insurance which covered the SMALLEST number of Americans under age 65 was

    A. hospital insurance
    B. surgical insurance
    C. insurance for prescription drugs
    D. insurance for physician office or home visits

14._____

Questions 15-17.

DIRECTIONS: Questions 15 through 17 are to be answered SOLELY on the basis of the information contained in the following passage.

Statistical studies have demonstrated that disease and mortality rates are higher among the poor than among the more affluent members of our society. Periodic surveys conducted by the United States Public Health Service continue to document a higher prevalence of infectious and chronic diseases within low income families. While the basic life style and living conditions of the poor are to a considerable extent responsible for this less favorable health status, there are indications that the kind of health care received by the poor also plays a significant role. The poor are less likely to be aware of the concepts and practices of scientific medicine and less likely to seek health care when they need it. Moreover, they are discouraged from seeking adequate health care by the depersonalization, disorganization, and inadequate emphasis on preventive care which characterize the health care most often provided for them.

To achieve the objective of better health care for the poor, the following approaches have been suggested: encouraging the poor to seek preventive care as well as care for acute illness and to establish a lasting one-to-one relationship with a single physician who can treat the poor patient as a whole individual; sufficient financial subsidy to put the poor on an equal footing with *paying patients,* thereby giving them the opportunity to choose from among available health services providers; inducements to health services providers to establish public clinics in poverty areas; and legislation to provide for health education, earlier detection of disease, and coordinated health care.

15. According to the above passage, the one of the following which is a function of the United States Public Health Service is

    A. gathering data on the incidence of infectious diseases
    B. operating public health clinics in poverty areas lacking private physicians
    C. recommending legislation for the improvement of health care in the United States
    D. encouraging the poor to participate in programs aimed at the prevention of illness

15._____

16. According to the above passage, the one of the following which is MOST characteristic of the health care currently provided for the poor is that it

    A. aims at establishing clinics in poverty areas
    B. enables the poor to select the health care they want through the use of financial subsidies
    C. places insufficient stress on preventive health care
    D. over-emphasizes the establishment of a one-to-one relationship between physician and patient

16.____

17. The above passage IMPLIES that the poor lack the financial resources to

    A. obtain adequate health insurance coverage
    B. select from among existing health services
    C. participate in health education programs
    D. lobby for legislation aimed at improving their health care

17.____

Questions 18-20.

DIRECTIONS: Questions 18 through 20 are to be answered SOLELY on the basis of the information contained in the following passage.

The concept of *affiliation,* developed more than ten years ago, grew out of a series of studies which found evidence of faulty care, surgery of *questionable* value and other undesirable conditions in the city's municipal hospitals. The affiliation agreements signed shortly thereafter were designed to correct these deficiencies by assuring high quality medical care. In general, the agreements provided the staff and expertise of a voluntary hospital—sometimes connected with a medical school—to operate various services or, in some cases, all of the professional divisions of a specific municipal hospital. The municipal hospitals have paid for these services, which last year cost the city $200 million, the largest single expenditure of the Health and Hospitals Corporation. In addition, the municipal hospitals have provided to the voluntary hospitals such facilities as free space for laboratories and research. While some experts agree that affiliation has resulted in improvements in some hospital care, they contend that many conditions that affiliation was meant to correct still exist. In addition, accountability procedures between the Corporation and voluntary hospitals are said to be so inadequate that audits of affiliation contracts of the past five years revealed that there may be more than $200 million in charges for services by the voluntary hospitals which have not been fully substantiated. Consequently, the Corporation has proposed that future agreements provide accountability in terms of funds, services supplied, and use of facilities by the voluntary hospitals.

18. According to the above passage, *affiliation* may BEST be defined as an agreement whereby

    A. voluntary hospitals pay for the use of municipal hospital facilities
    B. voluntary and municipal hospitals work to eliminate duplication of services
    C. municipal hospitals pay voluntary hospitals for services performed
    D. voluntary and municipal hospitals transfer patients to take advantage of specialized services

18.____

19. According to the above passage, the MAIN purpose for setting up the *affiliation* agreement was to

    A. supplement the revenues of municipal hospitals
    B. improve the quality of medical care in municipal hospitals
    C. reduce operating costs in municipal hospitals
    D. increase the amount of space available to municipal hospitals

19.___

20. According to the above passage, inadequate accountability procedures have resulted in

    A. unsubstantiated charges for services by the voluntary hospitals
    B. emphasis on research rather than on patient care in municipal hospitals
    C. unsubstantiated charges for services by the municipal hospitals
    D. economic losses to voluntary hospitals

20.___

Questions 21-25.

DIRECTIONS: Questions 21 through 25 are to be answered SOLELY on the basis of the information contained in the following passage.

The payment for medical services covered under the Outpatient Medical Insurance Plan (OMI) may be made, by OMI, directly to a physician or to the OMI patient. If the physician and the patient agree that the physician is to receive payment directly from OMI, the payment will be officially assigned to the physician; this is the assignment method. If payment is not assigned, the patient receives payment directly from OMI based on an itemized bill he submits, regardless of whether or not he has already paid his physician.

When a physician accepts assignment of the payment for medical services, he agrees that total charges will not be more than the allowed charge determined by the OMI carrier administering the program. In such cases, the OMI patient pays any unmet part of the $85 annual deductible, plus 10 percent of the remaining charges to the physician. In unassigned claims, the patient is responsible for the total amount charged by the physician. The patient will then be reimbursed by the program 90 percent of the allowed charges in excess of the annual deductible.

The rates of acceptance of assignments provide a measure of how many OMI patients are spared *administrative participation* in the program. Because physicians are free to accept or reject assignments, the rate in which assignments are made provide a general indication of the medical community's satisfaction with the OMI program, especially with the level of amounts paid by the program for specific services and the promptness of payment.

21. According to the above passage, in order for a physician to receive payment directly from OMI for medical services to an OMI patient, the physician would have to accept the assignment of payment, to have the consent of the patient, AND to

    A. submit to OMI a paid itemized bill
    B. collect from the patient 90% of the total bill
    C. collect from the patient the total amount of the charges for his services, a portion of which he will later reimburse the patient
    D. agree that his charges for services to the patient will not exceed the amount allowed by the program

21.___

22. According to the above passage, if a physician accepts assignment of payment, the patient pays

    22.____

    A. the total amount charged by the physician and is reimbursed by the program for 90 percent of the allowed charges in excess of the applicable deductible
    B. any unmet part of the $85 annual deductible, plus 90 percent of the remaining charges
    C. the total amount charged by the physician and is reimbursed by the program for 10 percent of the allowed charges in excess of the $85 annual deductible
    D. any unmet part of the $85 annual deductible, plus 10 percent of the remaining charges

23. A physician has accepted the assignment of payment for charges to an OMI patient. The physician's charges, all of which are allowed under OMI, amount to $115. This is the first time the patient has been eligible for OMI benefits and the first time the patient has received services from this physician.
    According to the above passage, the patient must pay the physician

    23.____

    A. $27   B. $76.50   C. $88   D. $103.50

24. In an unassigned claim, a physician's charges, all of which are allowed under OMI, amount to $165. The patient paid the physician the full amount of the bill.
    If this is the FIRST time the patient has been eligible for OMI benefits, he will receive from OMI a reimbursement of

    24.____

    A. $72   B. $80   C. $85   D. $93

25. According to the above passage, if the rate of acceptance of assignments by physicians is high, it is LEAST appropriate to conclude that the medical community is generally satisfied with the

    25.____

    A. supplementary medical insurance program
    B. levels of amounts paid to physicians by the program
    C. number of OMI patients being spared administrative participation in the program
    D. promptness of the program in making payment for services

_____

KEY (CORRECT ANSWERS)

1. B	11. C	21. D
2. A	12. A	22. D
3. C	13. C	23. C
4. D	14. D	24. A
5. A	15. A	25. C
6. D	16. C	
7. B	17. B	
8. C	18. C	
9. B	19. B	
10. D	20. A	

_____

READING COMPREHENSION
UNDERSTANDING AND INTERPRETING WRITTEN MATERIAL
EXAMINATION SECTION
TEST 1

DIRECTIONS: Each question or incomplete statement is followed by several suggested answers or completions. Select the one that BEST answers the question or completes the statement. *PRINT THE LETTER OF THE CORRECT ANSWER IN THE SPACE AT THE RIGHT.*

Questions 1-8.

DIRECTIONS: Questions 1 through 8 are to be answered on the basis of the following statement.

The child lives in a context which is itself neither simple nor unitary and which continuously affects his behavior and development. Patterns of stimulation come to him out of this context. In turn, by virtue of his own make-up, he selects from that context. At all times, there is a reciprocal relation between the human organism and this biosocial context. Because the child is limited in time, behavior becomes structured, and patterns develop both in the stimulus field and in his own response system. Some stimulus patterns become significant because they modify the developmental stream by affecting practice or social relations with others. Others remain insignificant because they do not affect this web of relations. Why one pattern is significant and another is not is a crucial problem for child psychology.

1. The author states that

    A. environmental forces have an important effect in determining both the child's actions and his course of growth
    B. environmental and hereditary forces play an equal part in determining both the child's actions and his course of growth
    C. even the environmental forces which are not consciously important to the child can affect both learning and personality
    D. the child's personality is shaped more by the total pattern of pressures in the environment

1._____

2. The author develops *context* so as to make it mean

    A. the nature of the child's immediate environment
    B. a complex rather than a simple home structure
    C. a multitude of past, present, and future forces
    D. internal as well as external influences

2._____

3. According to the author, the CRITICAL forces to be studied are those which

    A. are unconscious forces
    B. are conscious, unconscious, and subconscious forces
    C. cause the child to respond
    D. modify the child's interpersonal relationships

3._____

4. The author's point of view might BEST be labeled as

    A. environmentalist   B. behaviorist
    C. psychobiosocial   D. gestaltist

4._____

5. The author maintains that the environment

    A. is relatively stable
    B. is in a constant state of flux
    C. shows periods of marked instability
    D. is more stable than unstable

5._____

6. From the above paragraph, it is to be inferred that the

    A. child's personality is mechanistically determined by the nature of the environment
    B. unique interaction between the child and his environment shapes his personality
    C. child really shapes his own personality
    D. child's personality is more likely to be affected by than to affect the environment

6._____

7. By *structured behavior,* the author means

    A. conditioning of responses
    B. differentiated activity
    C. characteristic modes of reaction
    D. responses that have been modified by the developmental stream

7._____

8. The *patterns* to which the author refers are

    A. different for all children
    B. culturally determined mainly
    C. biologically determined mainly
    D. psychologically determined mainly

8._____

Questions 9-13.

DIRECTIONS: Questions 9 through 13 are to be answered on the basis of the following passage.

The Division of Child Guidance makes certain provisions for summer vacations for children receiving foster care. Foster parents wishing to take the child on a vacation within the United States must file Form CG-42 in duplicate at the office of the Division not later than 3 weeks prior to the starting date of the planned vacation. Such request must be approved in writing by the Social Investigator and the Assistant Supervisor. After the request has been approved, the original copy of Form CG-42 must be returned to the foster parents by the Social Investigator no later than 3 days prior to the planned starting date of the vacation. The city continues to pay the foster parents the standard rate for the child's care.

If the foster parents plan to take the child on a vacation outside the continental United States, Form CG-42 must be submitted in triplicate and must be received no later than 5 weeks prior to the starting date of the planned vacation. Such Form CG-42 for vacation outside the country must also be approved by the Case Supervisor. There will be no payment for time spent outside the United States.

When the approved original Form CG-42 is returned to the foster parents, it shall be accompanied by an original copy of Form CG-43. A duplicate copy of Form CG-43 shall be forwarded by the Case Supervisor to the Children's Accounts Section to stop payment for time expected to be spent outside the United States.

9. When a foster parent plans to take his foster child on a vacation trip, the Division of Child Guidance must receive Form

    9.____

    A. CG-42 in triplicate no later than five weeks prior to the scheduled start of his vacation trip to Canada

    B. CG-42 in duplicate no later than three weeks prior to the scheduled start of his vacation trip to Mexico

    C. CG-43 in triplicate no later than three weeks prior to the scheduled start of his vacation trip to Arizona

    D. CG-43 in duplicate no later than five weeks prior to the scheduled start of his vacation trip regardless of location

10. The one of the following steps which is required in processing a request from a foster parent to take a child on a vacation trip is that the

    10.____

    A. Case Supervisor send the original copy of Form CG-42 to the appropriate section in the case of a child who will spend all his vacation in a foreign country

    B. Children's Accounts Section receive the duplicate copy of Form CG-43 in the case of a child who will spend any part of his vacation in a foreign country

    C. Division of Child Guidance keep a permanent file of original copies of Form CG-43 to keep a control of all current vacation requests

    D. foster parents receive the triplicate copy of Form CG-42 from the Social Investigator in the case of a child who will spend part of his vacation in the United States

11. When a foster child spends an approved vacation with his foster father, payment for the child's care will be given to the foster father for

    11.____

    A. none of the time if part of the vacation is spent in a foreign country

    B. that part of the vacation spent inside the United States but a reduced daily rate

    C. the entire period at a standard rate if the vacation is spent wholly in the United States

    D. the entire time regardless of whether or not it is spent in a foreign country

12. The Division of Child Guidance must notify a foster parent that his request to take his foster child on a vacation outside the country has been approved by sending him the approved _____ copy of Form CG-42 and _____ copy of Form CG-43.

    12.____

    A. duplicate; duplicate
    B. duplicate; original
    C. original; duplicate
    D. original; original

13. On the basis of the above passage, children receiving foster care may be taken on a vacation trip by their foster parents to a location

    13.____

    A. anywhere in the world with the written approval of the Social Investigator only

    B. of the foster parents' choosing but only with the written approval of both the Assistant Supervisor and Case Supervisor

    C. outside the United States but only with the written approval of the Social Investigator, Assistant Supervisor, and Case Supervisor

    D. within the United States with the written approval of the Case Supervisor only

Questions 14-18.

DIRECTIONS: Questions 14 through 18 are statements based on the following paragraphs. For each question, there are two statements.

Based on the information in the paragraphs, mark your answer A, B, or C, as follows:
A, if only statement 1 is correct;
B, if only statement 2 is correct;
C, if both statements are correct.
Mark your answer D if the excerpts do not contain sufficient evidence for concluding whether either or both statements are correct.

Almost 49,000 children were living in foster family homes or voluntary institutions in the state at the end of 2003. These were children whose parents or relatives were unable or unwilling to care for them in their own homes. The State Department of Social Services supervised the care of these children served under the auspices of 64 social services districts and more than 150 private agencies and institutions. Almost 8 out of every 1,000 children 18 years of age or younger were in care away from their homes at the end of 2003. This estimate does not include a substantial, but unknown, number of children living outside their own homes who were placed there by their parents, relatives, or others without the assistance of a social agency.

The number of children in care (dependent, neglected, and delinquent combined) was up by 4,500 or 10 percent over the 2000-2003 period. Both the city and state reported similar increases. In the comparable period, the state's child population (18 years or less) rose only three percent. Thus, the foster care rate showed a moderate increase to 7.7 per thousand in 2003 from 7.2 thousand in 2000. The city's foster care rate in 2003, at 10.5 per thousand, was almost twice that for upstate New York, 5.7 per thousand. (Excluding delinquent children from the total in care in the state reduces the foster care rate per thousand to 7.2 in 2003 and the comparable 2000 figure to 6.7.)

Dependent and neglected children made up about 95 percent of the total number in foster family homes and voluntary institutions in the state at the end of 2003, as they did in 2000. Delinquent children sent into care (outside the state training school system) by the Family Court accounted for only 5 percent of the total. The number of delinquent children in care rose 5 percent, as an increase in the state, 28 percent, more than offset a 13 percent decline in the city. Delinquents comprised 4.9 percent of the total number of children in care upstate at the end of 2003 and 3.9 percent in the city.

14.   1. There were 45,000 children in care away from their own homes over the 2000-2003 period.   14._____
      2. The percentage decline of delinquent children in care in the city in 2003 was offset by a greater increase in the rest of the state.

15.   1. The increase in delinquent care rate in the state from 2000 to 2003 cannot be determined from the data given.   15._____
      2. The state's foster care rate in 2003, exclusive of the city, was about one-half the rate for the city.

16.   1. In 2000 and in 2003, the percentage of dependent and neglected children in foster   16.____
        family homes and voluntary institutions in the state was about the same.
     2. In 2000, the number of dependent and neglected children in foster family homes and
        voluntary institutions in the state was 43,250.

17.   1. The city's child population rose approximately three percent from 2000 to 2003.   17.____
     2. At the end of 2003, less than 1% of the children 18 years of age or younger were in
        care.

18.   1. Delinquents in the city comprised 4.4 percent of the total number of children in care in   18.____
        the city at the end of 2000.
     2. An unsubstantial number of children living outside their own homes were placed by
        their parents or relatives without the assistance of a social agency.

Questions 19-25.

DIRECTIONS: Questions 19 through 25 are to be answered SOLELY on the basis of the infor-
                mation contained in the following paragraph. Each question consists of a state-
                ment. You are to indicate whether the statement is TRUE (T) or FALSE (F).

RESPONSIBILITY OF PARENTS

     In a recent survey, ninety percent of the people interviewed felt that parents should be held
responsible for the delinquency of their children. Forty-eight out of fifty states have laws holding
parents criminally responsible for contributing to the delinquency of their children. It is generally
accepted that parents are a major influence in the early moral development of their children.
Yet, in spite of all this evidence, practical experience seems to prove that *punish the parents*
laws are wrong. Legally, there is some question about the constitutionality of such laws. How far
can one person be held responsible for the actions of another? Further, although there are
many such laws, the fact remains that they are rarely used and where they are used, they fail in
most cases to accomplish the end for which they were intended.

19.   Nine out of ten of those interviewed held that parents should be responsible for the delin-   19.____
    quency of their children.

20.   Forty-eight percent of the states have laws holding parents responsible for contributing to   20.____
    the delinquency of their children.

21.   Most people feel that parents have little influence on the early moral development of their   21.____
    children.

22.   Experience seems to indicate that laws holding parents responsible for children's delin-   22.____
    quency are wrong.

23.   There is no doubt that laws holding parents responsible for delinquency of their children   23.____
    are within the Constitution.

24.   Laws holding parents responsible for delinquent children are not often enforced.   24.____

25.   *Punish the parent* laws usually achieve their purpose.   25.____

KEY (CORRECT ANSWERS)

1.	A		11.	C
2.	D		12.	D
3.	D		13.	C
4.	C		14.	B
5.	B		15.	B
6.	B		16.	A
7.	C		17.	D
8.	A		18.	D
9.	A		19.	T
10.	B		20.	F

21.	F
22.	T
23.	F
24.	T
25.	F

TEST 2

DIRECTIONS: Each question or incomplete statement is followed by several suggested answers or completions. Select the one that BEST answers the question or completes the statement. *PRINT THE LETTER OF THE CORRECT ANSWER IN THE SPACE AT THE RIGHT.*

Questions 1-3.

DIRECTIONS: Questions 1 through 3 are to be answered SOLELY on the basis of the following passage.

Undoubtedly, the ultimate solution to the housing problem of the hard-core slum does not lie in code enforcement, however defined. The only solution to that problem is demolition, clearance, and new construction. However, it is also clear that, even with government assistance, new construction is not keeping pace with the obsolescence and deterioration of the existing housing inventory of our cities. Add to this the facts of an increasing population and the continuing migration into metropolitan areas, as well as the demands for more and better housing that grow out of continuing economic prosperity and high employment, and some intimation may be gained of the dimensions of the problem of maintaining our housing supply so that it may begin to meet the need.

1. The one of the following that would be the MOST appropriate title for the above passage is   1.____

    A. PROBLEMS ASSOCIATED WITH MAINTAINING AN ADEQUATE HOUSING SUPPLY
    B. DEMOLITION AS A REMEDY FOR HOUSING PROBLEMS
    C. GOVERNMENT'S ESSENTIAL ROLE IN CODE ENFORCEMENT
    D. THE ULTIMATE SOLUTION TO THE HARD-CORE SLUM PROBLEM

2. According to the above passage, housing code enforcement is   2.____

    A. a way to encourage local initiative in urban renewal
    B. a valuable tool that has fallen into disuse
    C. inadequate as a solution to slum housing problems
    D. responsible for some of the housing problems since the code has not been adequately defined

3. The above passage makes it clear that the BASIC solution to the housing problem is to   3.____

    A. erect new buildings after demolition and site clearance
    B. discourage migration into the metropolitan area
    C. increase rents paid to landlords
    D. enforce the housing code strictly

Questions 4-5.

DIRECTIONS: Questions 4 and 5 are to be answered SOLELY on the basis of the following passage.

Under common law, the tenant was obliged to continue to pay rent, at the risk of eviction, regardless of the condition of the premises. This obligation was based on the following established common law principles: first, that in the absence of express agreement, a lease does not contain any implied warranty of fitness or habitability; second, that the person in possession of premises has the obligation to repair and maintain them; and third, that a lease conveys an interest in real estate rather than binding one to a mutual obligation. Once having conveyed his property, the landlord's right to rent was unconditional. Thus, even if he made an express agreement to repair, the landlord's right to rent remained independent of his promise to repair. This doctrine, known as the *independence of covenants,* required the tenant to continue to pay rent or risk eviction, and to bring a separate action against the landlord for damages resulting from his breach of agreement to repair.

4. According to the above passage, common law provided that a lease would   4.____

   A. bar an ex parte action
   B. bind the parties thereto to a reciprocal obligation
   C. provide an absolute defense for breach of agreement
   D. transmit an interest in real property

5. According to the above passage, the *independence of covenants* required that the   5.____

   A. tenant continue to pay rent even for unfit housing
   B. landlord hold rents in escrow for aggrieved tenants
   C. landlord show valid cause for non-performance of lease requirements
   D. tenant surrender the demised premises in improved condition

Questions 6-11.

DIRECTIONS: Questions 6 through 11 are to be answered SOLELY on the basis of the information given in the following passage.

The City of X has set up a Maximum Base Rent Program for all rent-controlled apartments. The objective is to insure that the landlord will get a fair, but not excessive, profit on his building to stem the great tide of buildings being abandoned by their owners, and to encourage landlords to continue the upkeep of their property. The Maximum Base Rent Program permits the landlord to raise rents under carefully devised standards, while practically no raises in rents in this City were permitted under previous guidelines.

Under this plan, the City determines a Maximum Base Rent amount by means of a formula which takes into account the age of the building, the number of apartments, total rents received from the building, the amount of expenses, and labor costs. The Maximum Base Rent amount is to be recomputed every two years to allow for increases or decreases in building costs.

The Maximum Base Rent, which will allow the landlord to make a *fair return* on his investment, may not be collected immediately, however, since no rent increases over 7.5 percent will be permitted in any one year. The highest actual rent for each apartment during a given year will be called the Maximum Collectible Rent. This will be computed so that the increase over the present rent is not more than 7.5 percent ($7.50 on every $100.00). Sometimes, it may be less. Therefore, collectible rents will increase each year until the Maximum Base Rent is reached.

6. According to the above passage, the Maximum Base Rent is determined by the   6._____

    A. landlord   B. Mayor
    C. Rent Commissioner   D. City

7. Which of the following, according to the above passage, permits a *fair return* on the land-   7._____
    lord's investment?
    The _____ Rent Program.

    A. Minimum Base   B. Maximum Base
    C. Minimum Collectible   D. Maximum Collectible

8. It may be concluded from the above passage that the City of X hopes that insuring fair   8._____
    profits for landlords will be followed by

    A. good upkeep of apartment buildings
    B. decreased interest rates on home mortgages
    C. lower rents in the future
    D. a better formula for determining rents

9. According to the above passage, guidelines for determining rents previous to the Maxi-   9._____
    mum Base Rent Program resulted in

    A. practically no raises in rents being made
    B. rent increases of approximately 10 percent a year
    C. a *fair return* to landlords from most rents
    D. landlords making too much money on their property

10. Based on the above passage, which is the MOST correct description of the kinds of facts   10._____
    that are taken into consideration when determining the Maximum Base Rent? Facts
    about

    A. labor costs and politics
    B. the landlord and labor costs
    C. the building and labor costs
    D. the building and the landlord

11. According to the above passage, the MAXIMUM annual increase in rent for a tenant in   11._____
    rent-controlled housing under the Maximum Base Rent Program is

    A. 7.5 percent each year for ten years
    B. 7.5 percent each year until the Maximum Base Rent is reached
    C. always under 7.5 percent a year
    D. $7.50 each year until it reaches $100.00

Questions 12-15.

DIRECTIONS: Questions 12 through 15 are to be answered SOLELY on the basis of the infor-
               mation contained in the following paragraph.

    In all projects (except sites), when the Manager determines that a vacant apartment is to
be permanently removed from the rent roll for any reason, e.g., the apartment has been con-
verted to an office or community space, he shall notify the cashier by memorandum. The
cashier shall enter the reduction in dwelling units in the Rent Control Book as of the first of the

month following the date on which the apartment was vacated. He shall also prepare a reduction in Rent Roll (Form 105.046), the original of which is to be attached to the file copy of the Project Monthly Summary for the month during which the reduction is effective. Copies are to be sent to the Finance and Audit Department, Budget Section, and to the Chief of Insurance.

12. The purpose of the above paragraph is to provide for a procedure in handling   12._____

    A. the accounting for space occupied by offices and community centers
    B. apartments not rented as of the first of the month following the date on which the apartment was vacated
    C. vacant apartments temporarily used as office space
    D. vacant apartments permanently removed from the rent roll

13. The Rent Control Book is a control on the amount of monthly rents charged. According to the above paragraph, another function of the Rent Control Book is to indicate the   13._____

    A. number of offices and community spaces available in the project
    B. number of dwelling units in the project
    C. number of vacant apartments in the project
    D. rental loss for all offices and community spaces

14. In accordance with the above paragraph, the original of the Form 105.046 is to be   14._____

    A. sent to Central Office with the Project Monthly Summary
    B. kept in the project files with the project copy of the Project Monthly Summary
    C. sent to the Finance and Audit Department
    D. sent to the Chief of Insurance

15. The MOST likely reason for informing the Chief of Insurance of the removal of an apartment from the rent roll is to notify him   15._____

    A. to make adjustments in the insurance coverage
    B. of a future change in the address of the office or community space
    C. of a change in the project rent income
    D. of a possible increase in the number of project employees

Questions 16-20.

DIRECTIONS: Questions 16 through 20 are to be answered SOLELY on the basis of the information provided in the following passage.

It is the Housing Administration's policy that all tenants, whether new or transferring from one housing development to another, should be required to pay a standard security deposit of one month's rent based on the rent at the time of admission. There are, however, certain exceptions to this policy. Employees of the Administration shall not be required to pay a security deposit if they secure an apartment in an Administration development. Where the payment of a full security deposit may present a hardship to a tenant, the development's manager may allow a tenant to move into an apartment upon payment of only part of the security deposit. In such cases, however, the tenant must agree to gradually pay the balance of the deposit. If a tenant transfers from one apartment to another within the same project, the security deposit originally paid by the tenant for his former apartment will be acceptable for his new apartment, even if the rent in the new apartment is greater than the rent in the former one. Finally, tenants who receive public assistance need not pay a security deposit before moving into an apartment if the appropriate agency states, in writing, that it will pay the deposit. However, it is the responsibility of the development's manager to make certain that payment shall be received within one month of the date that the tenant moves into the apartment.

16. According to the above passage, when a tenant transfers from one apartment to another in the same development, the Housing Administration will   16.____

    A. accept the tenant's old security deposit as the security deposit for his new apartment regardless of the new apartment's rent
    B. refund the tenant's old security deposit and not require him to pay a new deposit
    C. keep the tenant's old security deposit and require him to pay a new deposit
    D. require the tenant to pay a new security deposit based on the difference between his old rent and his new rent

17. On the basis of the above passage, it is INCORRECT to state that a tenant who receives public assistance may move into an Administration development if   17.____

    A. he pays the appropriate security deposit
    B. the appropriate agency gives a written indication that it will pay the security deposit before the tenant moves in
    C. the appropriate agency states, by telephone, that it will pay the security deposit
    D. the appropriate agency writes the manager to indicate that the security deposit will be paid within one month but not less than two weeks from the date the tenant moves into the apartment

18. On the basis of the above passage, a tenant who transfers from an apartment in one development to an apartment in a different development will   18.____

    A. forfeit his old security deposit and be required to pay another deposit
    B. have his old security deposit refunded and not have to pay a new deposit
    C. pay the difference between his old security deposit and the new one
    D. have to pay a security deposit based on the new apartment's rent

19. The Housing Administration will NOT require payment of a security deposit if a tenant   19.____

    A. is an Administration employee
    B. is receiving public assistance
    C. claims that payment will present a hardship
    D. indicates, in writing, that he will be responsible for any damage done to his apartment

20. Of the following, the BEST title for the above passage is   20.____

    A. SECURITY DEPOSITS - TRANSFERS
    B. SECURITY DEPOSITS - POLICY
    C. EXEMPTIONS AND EXCEPTIONS - SECURITY DEPOSITS
    D. AMOUNTS - SECURITY DEPOSITS

Questions 21-23.

DIRECTIONS: Questions 21 through 23 are to be answered SOLELY on the basis of the following paragraphs.

In our program, we must continually strive to increase public good will and to maintain that good will which we have already established. It is important to remember in all your public contacts that to a good many people you are the Department. Don't take out any of your personal gripes on the public. When we must appeal to the public for cooperation, that is when any good will we have built up will come in handy. If the public has been given incorrect or incomplete help when seeking information or advice, or have received what they considered poor treatment in dealing with members of the Department, they will not provide a sympathetic audience when we direct our appeals to them.

One of the Department activities in which there is considerable contact with the public is inspection. Any activity in this area poses special problems and makes your personal dealings with the individuals involved very important. You must bear in mind that you are dealing with people who are sensitive to the manner in which they are treated and you should guide yourself accordingly.

Let us consider some of the aspects of the actual inspection of the premises:

APPEARANCE - Your appearance will determine the initial impression made on anyone you deal with. It is often difficult to change a person's first impression, so try to make it a favorable one. Be neat and clean; show that you have taken some trouble to make a good appearance. Your appearance should form a part of a business-like attitude that should govern your inspection of any premises.

APPROACH - Be courteous at all times. When you enter a building, immediately seek out the owner or occupant and ask his permission to inspect the premises. Ask him to accompany you on the inspection if he has the time, and explain to him the reasons why such inspections are made. Try to give him the feeling that this is a cooperative effort and that his part in this effort is appreciated. Do not make your approach on the basis that it is your legal right to inspect the premises; a <u>coercive</u> attitude tends to produce a hostile reaction.

21. Of the following, the BEST title for the subject covered in the above paragraphs is   21.____

    A. GOOD MANNERS   B. PUBLIC RELATIONS
    C. NEATNESS   D. INSPECTIONAL DUTIES

22. According to the above paragraphs, the FIRST impression an inspector makes on the   22.____
public is that of

    A. sympathy   B. courtesy
    C. cleanliness and dress   D. business attitude

23. According to the above paragraphs, if you want the public to cooperate with you, you   23.____
must

    A. be available at all times
    B. be sure that any information you give them is correct
    C. make sure that their complaints are justified
    D. be stern in your dealings with landlords

Questions 24-25.

DIRECTIONS: Questions 24 and 25 are to be answered SOLELY on the basis of the following passage.

There is no simple solution for controlling crime and deviant behavior. There is no panacea for anti-social conduct. The sooner society gives up the search for a single control solution, the sooner society will be able to face up to the immensity of the task and the never-ending responsibility of our social structure.

24. Which of the following statements is BEST supported by the above passage?

    A. Although crime causation may be considered singular, crime control is many-faceted.
    B. When society faces up to the immensity of the crime problem, it will find a single solution to it.
    C. A multi-faceted approach to crime control is better than trying to find a single cause or cure.
    D. Our social structure is responsible for a continuing search for a simple solution to anti-social behavior.

24.____

25. The crime problem can be solved when

    A. it is realized that no solution exists
    B. the problem is specifically identified
    C. criminals are punished
    D. none of the above

25.____

_____

KEY (CORRECT ANSWERS)

1.	A		11.	B
2.	C		12.	D
3.	A		13.	B
4.	D		14.	B
5.	A		15.	A
6.	D		16.	A
7.	B		17.	C
8.	A		18.	D
9.	A		19.	A
10.	C		20.	B

21.	B
22.	C
23.	B
24.	C
25.	D

_____

CLERICAL ABILITIES

EXAMINATION SECTION
TEST 1

DIRECTIONS: Each question or incomplete statement is followed by several suggested answers or completions. Select the one that BEST answers the question or completes the statement. *PRINT THE LETTER OF THE CORRECT ANSWER IN THE SPACE AT THE RIGHT.*

Questions 1-4.

DIRECTIONS: Questions 1 through 4 are to be answered on the basis of the information given below.

The most commonly used filing system and the one that is easiest to learn is alphabetical filing. This involves putting records in an A to Z order, according to the letters of the alphabet. The name of a person is filed by using the following order: first, the surname or last name; second, the first name; third, the middle name or middle initial. For example, *Henry C. Young* is filed under *Y* and thereafter under *Young, Henry C.* The name of a company is filed in the same way. For example, *Long Cabinet Co.* is filed under *L,* while *John T. Long Cabinet Co.* is filed under *L* and thereafter under *Long., John T. Cabinet Co.*

1. The one of the following which lists the names of persons in the CORRECT alphabetical order is:

    A. Mary Carrie, Helen Carrol, James Carson, John Carter
    B. James Carson, Mary Carrie, John Carter, Helen Carrol
    C. Helen Carrol, James Carson, John Carter, Mary Carrie
    D. John Carter, Helen Carrol, Mary Carrie, James Carson

1.____

2. The one of the following which lists the names of persons in the CORRECT alphabetical order is:

    A. Jones, John C.; Jones, John A.; Jones, John P.; Jones, John K.
    B. Jones, John P.; Jones, John K.; Jones, John C.; Jones, John A.
    C. Jones, John A.; Jones, John C.; Jones, John K.; Jones, John P.
    D. Jones, John K.; Jones, John C.; Jones, John A.; Jones, John P.

2.____

3. The one of the following which lists the names of the companies in the CORRECT alphabetical order is:

    A. Blane Co., Blake Co., Block Co., Blear Co.
    B. Blake Co., Blane Co., Blear Co., Block Co.
    C. Block Co., Blear Co., Blane Co., Blake Co.
    D. Blear Co., Blake Co., Blane Co., Block Co.

3.____

4. You are to return to the file an index card on *Barry C. Wayne Materials and Supplies Co.* Of the following, the CORRECT alphabetical group that you should return the index card to is

    A. A to G   B. H to M   C. N to S   D. T to Z

4.____

DIRECTIONS: In each of Questions 5 through 10, the names of four people are given. For each question, choose as your answer the one of the four names given which should be filed FIRST according to the usual system of alphabetical filing of names, as described in the following paragraph.

In filing names, you must start with the last name. Names are filed in order of the first letter of the last name, then the second letter, etc. Therefore, BAILY would be filed before BROWN, which would be filed before COLT. A name with fewer letters of the same type comes first; i.e., Smith before Smithe. If the last names are the same, the names are filed alphabetically by the first name. If the first name is an initial, a name with an initial would come before a first name that starts with the same letter as the initial. Therefore, I. BROWN would come before IRA BROWN. Finally, if both last name and first name are the same, the name would be filed alphabetically by the middle name, once again an initial coming before a middle name which starts with the same letter as the initial. If there is no middle name at all, the name would come before those with middle initials or names.

Sample Question: A.   Lester Daniels
                      B.   William Dancer
                      C.   Nathan Danzig
                      D.   Dan Lester

The last names beginning with D are filed before the last name beginning with L. Since DANIELS, DANCER, and DANZIG all begin with the same three letters, you must look at the fourth letter of the last name to determine which name should be filed first. C comes before I or Z in the alphabet, so DANCER is filed before DANIELS or DANZIG. Therefore, the answer to the above sample question is B.

5.   A.   Scott Biala
    B.   Mary Byala
    C.   Martin Baylor
    D.   Francis Bauer

5._____

6.   A.   Howard J. Black
    B.   Howard Black
    C.   J. Howard Black
    D.   John H. Black

6._____

7.   A.   Theodora Garth Kingston
    B.   Theadore Barth Kingston
    C.   Thomas Kingston
    D.   Thomas T. Kingston

7._____

8.   A.   Paulette Mary Huerta
    B.   Paul M. Huerta
    C.   Paulette L. Huerta
    D.   Peter A. Huerta

8._____

9.   A.   Martha Hunt Morgan
     B.   Martin Hunt Morgan
     C.   Mary H. Morgan
     D.   Martine H. Morgan

9._____

10.   A.   James T. Meerschaum
     B.   James M. Mershum
     C.   James F. Mearshaum
     D.   James N. Meshum

10._____

Questions 11-14.

DIRECTIONS: Questions 11 through 14 are to be answered SOLELY on the basis of the following information.

You are required to file various documents in file drawers which are labeled according to the following pattern:

DOCUMENTS

MEMOS		LETTERS	
File	Subject	File	Subject
84PM1 - (A-L)		84PC1 - (A-L)	
84PM2 - (M-Z)		84PC2 - (M-Z)	

REPORTS		INQUIRIES	
File	Subject	File	Subject
84PR1 - (A-L)		84PQ1 - (A-L)	
84PR2 - (M-Z)		84PQ2 - (M-Z)	

11.   A letter dealing with a burglary should be filed in the drawer labeled

    A.   84PM1   B.   84PC1   C.   84PR1   D.   84PQ2

11._____

12.   A report on Statistics should be found in the drawer labeled

    A.   84PM1   B.   84PC2   C.   84PR2   D.   84PQ2

12._____

13.   An inquiry is received about parade permit procedures. It should be filed in the drawer labeled

    A.   84PM2   B.   84PC1   C.   84PR1   D.   84PQ2

13._____

14.   A police officer has a question about a robbery report you filed.
You should pull this file from the drawer labeled

    A.   84PM1   B.   84PM2   C.   84PR1   D.   84PR2

14._____

Questions 15-22.

DIRECTIONS: Each of Questions 15 through 22 consists of four or six numbered names. For each question, choose the option (A, B, C, or D) which indicates the order in which the names should be filed in accordance with the following filing instructions:
- File alphabetically according to last name, then first name, then middle initial.
- File according to each successive letter within a name.

- When comparing two names in which, the letters in the longer name are identical to the corresponding letters in the shorter name, the shorter name is filed first.
- When the last names are the same, initials are always filed before names beginning with the same letter.

15.   I.   Ralph Robinson   15.____
            II. Alfred Ross
          III. Luis Robles
         IV. James Roberts

The CORRECT filing sequence for the above names should be

A. IV, II, I, III   B. I, IV, III, II
C. III, IV, I, II   D. IV, I, III, II

16.   I.   Irwin Goodwin   16.____
            II. Inez Gonzalez
          III. Irene Goodman
         IV. Ira S. Goodwin
          V. Ruth I. Goldstein
        VI. M.B. Goodman

The CORRECT filing sequence for the above names should be

A. V, II, I, IV, III, VI   B. V, II, VI, III, IV, I
C. V, II, III, VI, IV, I   D. V, II, III, VI, I, IV

17.   I.   George Allan   17.____
            II. Gregory Allen
          III. Gary Allen
         IV. George Allen

The CORRECT filing sequence for the above names should be

A. IV, III, I, II   B. I, IV, II, III
C. III, IV, I, II   D. I, III, IV, II

18.   I.   Simon Kauffman   18.____
            II. Leo Kaufman
          III. Robert Kaufmann
         IV. Paul Kauffmann

The CORRECT filing sequence for the above names should be

A. I, IV, II, III   B. II, IV, III, I
C. III, II, IV, I   D. I, II, III, IV

19.   I.   Roberta Williams   19.____
            II. Robin Wilson
          III. Roberta Wilson
         IV. Robin Williams

The CORRECT filing sequence for the above names should be

A. III, II, IV, I   B. I, IV, III, II
C. I, II, III, IV   D. III, I, II, IV

20.
    I.   Lawrence Shultz
    II.   Albert Schultz
    III. Theodore Schwartz
    IV. Thomas Schwarz
    V.   Alvin Schultz
    VI. Leonard Shultz

20.____

The CORRECT filing sequence for the above names should be

A. II, V, III, IV, I, VI
C. II, V, I, VI, III, IV

B. IV, III, V, I, II, VI
D. I, VI, II, V, III, IV

21.
    I.   McArdle
    II.   Mayer
    III. Maletz
    IV. McNiff
    V.   Meyer
    VI. MacMahon

21.____

The CORRECT filing sequence for the above names should be

A. I, IV, VI, III, II, V
C. VI, III, II, I, IV, V

B. II, I, IV, VI, III, V
D. VI, III, II, V, I, IV

22.
    I.   Jack E. Johnson
    II.   R.H. Jackson
    III. Bertha Jackson
    IV. J.T. Johnson
    V.   Ann Johns
    VI. John Jacobs

22.____

The CORRECT filing sequence for the above names should be

A. II, III, VI, V, IV, I
C. VI, II, III, I, V, IV

B. III, II, VI, V, IV, I
D. III, II, VI, IV, V, I

Questions 23-30.

DIRECTIONS: The code table below shows 10 letters with matching numbers. For each question, there are three sets of letters. Each set of letters is followed by a set of numbers which may or may not match their correct letter according to the code table. For each question, check all three sets of letters and numbers and mark your answer:
    A. if no pairs are correctly matched
    B. if only one pair is correctly matched
    C. if only two pairs are correctly matched
    D. if all three pairs are correctly matched

CODE TABLE

T	M	V	D	S	P	R	G	B	H
1	2	3	4	5	6	7	8	9	0

<u>Sample Question:</u>   TMVDSP - 123456
                       RGBHTM - 789011
                       DSPRGB - 256789

In the sample question above, the first set of numbers correctly matches its set of letters. But the second and third pairs contain mistakes. In the second pair, M is incorrectly matched with number 1. According to the code table, letter M should be correctly matched with number 2. In the third pair, the letter D is incorrectly matched with number 2. According to the code table, letter D should be correctly matched with number 4. Since only one of the pairs is correctly matched, the answer to this sample question is B.

23. RSBMRM 759262
     GDSRVH 845730
     VDBRTM 349713

23.____

24. TGVSDR 183247
     SMHRDP 520647
     TRMHSR 172057

24.____

25. DSPRGM 456782
     MVDBHT 234902
     HPMDBT 062491

25.____

26. BVPTRD 936184
     GDPHMB 807029
     GMRHMV 827032

26.____

27. MGVRSH 283750
     TRDMBS 174295
     SPRMGV 567283

27.____

28. SGBSDM 489542
     MGHPTM 290612
     MPBMHT 269301

28.____

29. TDPBHM 146902
     VPBMRS 369275
     GDMBHM 842902

29.____

30. MVPTBV 236194
     PDRTMB 647128
     BGTMSM 981232

30.____

_____

KEY (CORRECT ANSWERS)

1.	A	11.	B	21.	C
2.	C	12.	C	22.	B
3.	B	13.	D	23.	B
4.	D	14.	D	24.	B
5.	D	15.	D	25.	C
6.	B	16.	C	26.	A
7.	B	17.	D	27.	D
8.	B	18.	A	28.	A
9.	A	19.	B	29.	D
10.	C	20.	A	30.	A

———

TEST 2

DIRECTIONS: Each question or incomplete statement is followed by several suggested answers or completions. Select the one that BEST answers the question or completes the statement. *PRINT THE LETTER OF THE CORRECT ANSWER IN THE SPACE AT THE RIGHT.*

Questions 1-10.

DIRECTIONS: Questions 1 through 10 each consists of two columns, each containing four lines of names, numbers and/or addresses. For each question, compare the lines in Column I with the lines in Column II to see if they match exactly, and mark your answer A, B, C, or D, according to the following instructions:
- A. all four lines match exactly
- B. only three lines match exactly
- C. only two lines match exactly
- D. only one line matches exactly

	COLUMN I	COLUMN II	
1.	I. Earl Hodgson II. 1409870 III. Shore Ave. IV. Macon Rd.	Earl Hodgson 1408970 Schore Ave. Macon Rd.	1.____
2.	I. 9671485 II. 470 Astor Court III. Halprin, Phillip IV. Frank D. Poliseo	9671485 470 Astor Court Halperin, Phillip Frank D. Poliseo	2.____
3.	I. Tandem Associates II. 144-17 Northern Blvd. III. Alberta Forchi IV. Kings Park, NY 10751	Tandom Associates 144-17 Northern Blvd. Albert Forchi Kings Point, NY 10751	3.____
4.	I. Bertha C. McCormack II. Clayton, MO. III. 976-4242 IV. New City, NY 10951	Bertha C. McCormack Clayton, MO. 976-4242 New City, NY 10951	4.____
5.	I. George C. Morill II. Columbia, SC 29201 III. Louis Ingham IV. 3406 Forest Ave.	George C. Morrill Columbia, SD 29201 Louis Ingham 3406 Forest Ave.	5.____
6.	I. 506 S. Elliott Pl. II. Herbert Hall III. 4712 Rockaway Pkway IV. 169 E. 7 St.	506 S. Elliott Pl. Hurbert Hall 4712 Rockaway Pkway 169 E. 7 St.	6.____

	COLUMN I	COLUMN II	
7.	I. 345 Park Ave. II. Colman Oven Corp. III. Robert Conte IV. 6179846	345 Park Pl. Coleman Oven Corp. Robert Conti 6179846	7.____
8.	I. Grigori Schierber II. Des Moines, Iowa III. Gouverneur Hospital IV. 91-35 Cresskill Pl.	Grigori Schierber Des Moines, Iowa Gouverneur Hospital 91-35 Cresskill Pl.	8.____
9.	I. Jeffery Janssen II. 8041071 III. 40 Rockefeller Plaza IV. 407 6 St.	Jeffrey Janssen 8041071 40 Rockafeller Plaza 406 7 St.	9.____
10.	I. 5971996 II. 3113 Knickerbocker Ave. III. 8434 Boston Post Rd. IV. Penn Station	5871996 3113 Knickerbocker Ave. 8424 Boston Post Rd. Penn Station	10.____

Questions 11-14.

DIRECTIONS: Questions 11 through 14 are to be answered by looking at the four groups of names and addresses listed below (I, II, III, and IV) and then finding out the number of groups that have their corresponding numbered lines exactly the same.

	GROUP I	GROUP II
Line 1.	Richmond General Hospital	Richman General Hospital
Line 2.	Geriatric Clinic	Geriatric Clinic
Line 3.	3975 Paerdegat St.	3975 Peardegat St.
Line 4	Loudonville, New York 11538	Londonville, New York 11538

	GROUP III	GROUP IV
Line 1.	Richmond General Hospital	Richmend General Hospital
Line 2.	Geriatric Clinic	Geriatric Clinic
Line 3.	3795 Paerdegat St.	3975 Paerdegat St.
Line 4.	Loudonville, New York 11358	Loudonville, New York 11538

11. In how many groups is line one exactly the same?   11.____

    A. Two   B. Three   C. Four   D. None

12. In how many groups is line two exactly the same?   12.____

    A. Two   B. Three   C. Four   D. None

13. In how many groups is line three exactly the same?   13.____

    A. Two   B. Three   C. Four   D. None

14. In how many groups is line four exactly the same? 14.____

    A. Two   B. Three   C. Four   D. None

Questions 15-18.

DIRECTIONS: Each of Questions 15 through 18 has two lists of names and addresses. Each list contains three sets of names and addresses. Check each of the three sets in the list on the right to see if they are the same as the corresponding set in the list on the left. Mark your answers:
- A. if none of the sets in the right list are the same as those in the left list
- B. if only one of the sets in the right list is the same as those in the left list
- C. if only two of the sets in the right list are the same as those in the left list
- D. if all three sets in the right list are the same as those in the left list

15.
    Mary T. Berlinger   Mary T. Berlinger   15.____
    2351 Hampton St.   2351 Hampton St.
    Monsey, N.Y. 20117   Monsey, N.Y. 20117

    Eduardo Benes   Eduardo Benes
    473 Kingston Avenue   473 Kingston Avenue
    Central Islip, N.Y. 11734   Central Islip, N.Y. 11734

    Alan Carrington Fuchs   Alan Carrington Fuchs
    17 Gnarled Hollow Road   17 Gnarled Hollow Road
    Los Angeles, CA 91635   Los Angeles, CA 91685

16.
    David John Jacobson   David John Jacobson   16.____
    178 35 St. Apt. 4C   178 53 St. Apt. 4C
    New York, N.Y. 00927   New York, N.Y. 00927

    Ann-Marie Calonella   Ann-Marie Calonella
    7243 South Ridge Blvd.   7243 South Ridge Blvd.
    Bakersfield, CA 96714   Bakersfield, CA 96714

    Pauline M. Thompson   Pauline M. Thomson
    872 Linden Ave.   872 Linden Ave.
    Houston, Texas 70321   Houston, Texas 70321

17.
    Chester LeRoy Masterton   Chester LeRoy Masterson   17.____
    152 Lacy Rd.   152 Lacy Rd.
    Kankakee, Ill. 54532   Kankakee, Ill. 54532

    William Maloney   William Maloney
    S. LaCrosse Pla.   S. LaCross Pla.
    Wausau, Wisconsin 52146   Wausau, Wisconsin 52146

    Cynthia V. Barnes   Cynthia V. Barnes
    16 Pines Rd.   16 Pines Rd.
    Greenpoint, Miss. 20376   Greenpoint, Miss. 20376

18.   Marcel Jean Frontenac   Marcel Jean Frontenac   18._____
        8 Burton On The Water   6 Burton On The Water
        Calender, Me. 01471   Calender, Me. 01471

        J. Scott Marsden   J. Scott Marsden
        174 S. Tipton St.   174 Tipton St.
        Cleveland, Ohio   Cleveland, Ohio

        Lawrence T. Haney   Lawrence T. Haney
        171 McDonough St.   171 McDonough St.
        Decatur, Ga. 31304   Decatur, Ga. 31304

Questions 19-26.

DIRECTIONS: Each of Questions 19 through 26 has two lists of numbers. Each list contains three sets of numbers. Check each of the three sets in the list on the right to see if they are the same as the corresponding set in the list on the left. Mark your answers:

    A.   if none of the sets in the right list are the same as those in the left list
    B.   if only one of the sets in the right list is the same as those in the left list
    C.   if only two of the sets in the right list are the same as those in the left list
    D.   if all three sets in the right list are the same as those in the left list

19. 7354183476   7354983476   19._____
     4474747744   4474747774
     57914302311   57914302311

20. 7143592185   7143892185   20._____
     8344517699   8344518699
     9178531263   9178531263

21. 2572114731   257214731   21._____
     8806835476   8806835476
     8255831246   8255831246

22. 331476853821   331476858621   22._____
     6976658532996   6976655832996
     3766042113715   3766042113745

23. 8806663315   8806663315   23._____
     74477138449   74477138449
     211756663666   211756663666

24. 990006966996   99000696996   24._____
     53022219743   53022219843
     4171171117717   4171171177717

25. 24400222433004   24400222433004   25._____
     5300030055000355   5300030055500355
     20000075532002022   20000075532002022

26. 611166640660001116
    711130011700110073 3
    26666446664476518
    611166640660001116
    711130011700110073 3
    26666446664476518
    26._____

Questions 27-30.

DIRECTIONS: Questions 27 through 30 are to be answered by picking the answer which is in the correct numerical order, from the lowest number to the highest number, in each question.

27. A. 44533, 44518, 44516, 44547
    B. 44516, 44518, 44533, 44547
    C. 44547, 44533, 44518, 44516
    D. 44518, 44516, 44547, 44533
    27._____

28. A. 95587, 95593, 95601, 95620
    B. 95601, 95620, 95587, 95593
    C. 95593, 95587, 95601, 95620
    D. 95620, 95601, 95593, 95587
    28._____

29. A. 232212, 232208, 232232, 232223
    B. 232208, 232223, 232212, 232232
    C. 232208, 232212, 232223, 232232
    D. 232223, 232232, 232208, 232212
    29._____

30. A. 113419, 113521, 113462, 113588
    B. 113588, 113462, 113521, 113419
    C. 113521, 113588, 113419, 113462
    D. 113419, 113462, 113521, 113588
    30._____

KEY (CORRECT ANSWERS)

1.	C	11.	A	21.	C
2.	B	12.	C	22.	A
3.	D	13.	A	23.	D
4.	A	14.	A	24.	A
5.	C	15.	C	25.	C
6.	B	16.	B	26.	C
7.	D	17.	B	27.	B
8.	A	18.	B	28.	A
9.	D	19.	B	29.	C
10.	C	20.	B	30.	D

CODING
EXAMINATION SECTION

COMMENTARY

An ingenious question-type called coding, involving elements of alphabetizing, filing, name and number comparison, and evaluative judgement and application, has currently won wide acceptance in testing circles for measuring clerical aptitude and general ability, particularly on the senior (middle) grades (levels).

While the directions for this question usually vary in detail, the candidate is generally asked to consider groups of names, codes, and numbers, and then, according to a given plan, to arrange codes in alphabetic order; to arrange these in numerical sequence; to re-arrange columns of names and numbers in correct order; to espy errors in coding; to choose the correct coding arrangement in consonance with the given directions and examples, etc.

This question-type appears to have few parameters in respect to form, substance, or degree of difficulty.

Accordingly acquaintance with, and practice in, the coding question is recommended for the serious candidate.

TEST 1

DIRECTIONS: Answer questions 1 through 8 an the basis of the code table and the instructions given below.

Code Letter for Traffic Problem	B	H	Q	J	F	L	M	I
Code Number for Action Taken	1	2	3	4	5	6	7	8

Assume that each of the capital letters on the above chart is a radio code for a particular traffic problem and that the number immediately below each capital letter is the radio code for the correct action to be taken to deal with the problem. For instance, "1" is the action to be taken to deal with problem "B", "2" is the action to be taken to deal with problem "H", and so forth.

In each question, a series of code letters is given in Column 1. Column 2 gives four different arrangements of code numbers. You are to pick the answer (A, B, C, or D) in Column 2 that gives the code numbers that match the code letters in the same order

SAMPLE QUESTION

<u>Column 1</u>
BHLFMQ

<u>Column 2</u>
A. 125678
B. 216573
C. 127653
D. 126573

According to the chart, the code numbers that correspond to these code letters are as follows: B - 1, M - 2, L - 6, F - 5, M - 7, Q - 3. Therefore, the right answer is 126573. This answer is D in Column 2.

Column 1	Column 2	
1. BHQLMI	A. 123456 B. 123567 C. 123678 D. 125678	1.____
2. HBJQLF	A. 214365 B. 213456 C. 213465 D. 214387	2.____
3. QHMLFJ	A. 321654 B. 345678 C. 327645 D. 327654	3.____
4. FLQJIM	A. 543287 B. 563487 C. 564378 D. 654378	4.____
5. FBIHMJ	A. 518274 B. 152874 C. 528164 D. 517842	5.____
6. MIHFQB	A. 872341 B. 782531 C. 782341 D. 783214	6.____
7. JLFHQIM	A. 465237 B. 456387 C. 4652387 D. 4562387	7.____
8. LBJQIFH	A. 6143852 B. 6134852 C. 61437852 D. 61431852	8.____

KEY (CORRECT ANSWERS)

1.	C	5.	A
2.	A	6.	B
3.	D	7.	C
4.	B	8.	A

TEST 2

DIRECTIONS: Questions 1 through 5 are based on the following list showing the name and number of each of nine inmates.

1. Johnson	4. Thompson	7. Gordon
2. Smith	5. Frank	8. Porter
3. Edwards	6. Murray	9. Lopez

Each question consists of 3 sets of numbers and letters. Each set should consist of the numbers of three inmates and the first letter of each of their names. The letters should be in the same order as the numbers. In at least two of the three choices, there will be an error. On your answer sheet, mark only that choice in which the letters correspond with the numbers and are in the same order. If all three sets are wrong, mark choice D in your answer space.

SAMPLE QUESTION
A. 386 EPM
B. 542 FST
C. 474 LGT

Since 3 corresponds to E for Edwards, 8 corresponds to P for Porter, and 6 corresponds to M for Murray, choice A is correct and should be entered in your answer space. Choice B is wrong because letters T and S have been reversed. Choice C is wrong because the first number, which is 4, does *NOT* correspond with the first letter of choice C, which is L. It should have been T. If choice A were also wrong, then D would be the correct answer.

1. A. 382 EGS	B. 461 TMJ	C. 875 PLF		1.____
2. A. 549 FLT	B. 692 MJS	C. 758 GSP		2.____
3. A. 936 LEM	B. 253 FSE	C. 147 JTL		3.____
4. A. 569 PML	B. 716 GJP	C. 842 PTS		4.____
5. A. 356 FEM	B. 198 JPL	C. 637 MEG		5.____

Questions 6-10

DIRECTIONS: Answer questions 6 through 10 on the basis of the following information:

In order to make sure stock is properly located, incoming units are stored as follows:

STOCK NUMBERS		BIN NUMBERS	
00100	- 39999	D30,	L44
40000	- 69999	I4L,	D38
70000	- 99999	41L,	80D
100000 and over		614,	83D

Using the above table, choose the answer A, B, C, or D, which lists the correct Bin Number for the Stock Number given

6. 17243   6.____
    A. 41L   B. 83D   C. I4L   D. D30

7. 9219   7.____
    A. D38   B. L44   C. 614   D. 41L

8. 90125   8.____
    A. 41L   B. 614   C. D38   D. D30

9. 10001   9.____
    A. L44   B. D38   C. 80D   D. 83D

10. 200100   10.____
    A. 41L   B. I4L   C. 83D   D. D30

_____

KEY (CORRECT ANSWERS)

1. B
2. D
3. A
4. C
5. C

6. D
7. B
8. A
9. A
10. C

_____

TEST 3

DIRECTIONS: Assume that the Police Department is planning to conduct a statistical study of individuals who have been convicted of crimes during a certain year. For the purpose of this study, identification numbers are being assigned to individuals in the following manner:

The first two digits indicate the age of the individual:
The third digit indicates the sex of the individual:
    1.   male
    2.   female

The fourth digit indicates the type of crime involved:
    1.   criminal homicide
    2.   forcible rape
    3.   robbery
    4.   aggravated assault
    5.   burglary
    6.   larceny
    7.   auto theft
    8.   other

The fifth and sixth digits indicate the month in which the conviction occurred:
    01.   January
    02.   February, etc.

Answer questions 1 through 9 *SOLELY* on the basis of the above information and the following list of individuals and identification numbers.

Abbott, Richard	271304	Morris, Chris	212705
Collins, Terry	352111	Owens, William	231412
Elders, Edward	191207	Parker, Leonard	291807
George, Linda	182809	Robinson, Charles	311102
Hill, Leslie	251702	Sands, Jean	202610
Jones , Jackie	301106	Smith, Michael	421308
Lewis, Edith	402406	Turner, Donald	191601
Mack, Helen	332509	White, Barbara	242803

1.   The number of women on the above list is   1._____

    A. 6   B. 7   C. 8   D. 9

2.   The two convictions which occurred during February were for the crimes of   2._____

    A.   aggravated assault and auto theft
    B.   auto theft and criminal homicide
    C.   burglary and larceny
    D.   forcible rape and robbery

3.   The *ONLY* man convicted of auto theft was   3._____

    A.   Richard Abbott   B.   Leslie Hill
    C.   Chris Morris   D.   Leonard Parker

4. The number of people on the list who were 25 years old or older is

   A. 6   B. 7   C. 8   D. 9

4._____

5. The *OLDEST* person on the list is

   A. Terry Collins   B. Edith Lewis
   C. Helen Mack   D. Michael Smith

5._____

6. The two people on the list who are the same age are

   A. Richard Abbott and Michael Smith
   B. Edward Elders and Donald Turner
   C. Linda George and Helen Mack
   D. Leslie Hill and Charles Robinson

6._____

7. A 28-year-old man who was convicted of aggravated assault in October would have identification number

   A. 281410   B. 281509   C. 282311   D. 282409

7._____

8. A 33-year-old woman convicted in April of criminal homicide would have identification number

   A. 331140   B. 331204   C. 332014   D. 332104

8._____

9. The number of people on the above list who were convicted during the first six months of the year is

   A. 6   B. 7   C. 8   D. 9

9._____

Questions 10-19.

DIRECTIONS: The following is a list of patients who were referred by various clinics to the laboratory for tests. After each name is a patient identification number. Answer questions 10 through 19 based on the information contained in this list and the explanation accompanying it.

The *first digit* refers to the clinic which made the referral:

   1. Cardiac   6. Hematology
   2. Renal   7. Gynecology
   3. Pediatrics   8. Neurology
   4. Opthalmology   9. Gastroenterology
   5. Orthopedics

The *second digit* refers to the sex of the patient:

   1. male   2. female

The *third* and *fourth digits* give the age of the patient.

The *last two digits give* the day of the month the laboratory tests were performed.

LABORATORY REFERRALS DURING JANUARY

Adams, Jacqueline	320917	Miller, Michael	511806
Black, Leslie	813406	Pratt, William	214411
Cook, Marie	511616	Rogers, Ellen	722428
Fisher, Pat	914625	Saunders, Sally	310229
Jackson, Lee	923212	Wilson, Jan	416715
James, Linda	624621	Wyatt, Mark	321326
Lane, Arthur	115702		

10. According to the list, the number of women referred to the laboratory during January was   10._____

   A. 4   B. 5   C. 6   D. 7

11. The clinic from which the MOST patients were referred was   11._____

   A. Cardiac   B. Gynecology
   C. Opthamology   D. Pediatrics

12. The YOUNGEST patient referred from any clinic other than Pediatrics was   12._____

   A. Leslie Black   B. Marie Cook
   C. Arthur Lane   D. Sally Saunders

13. The number of patients whose laboratory tests were performed on or before January 16   13._____
    was

   A. 7   B. 8   C. 9   D. 10

14. The number of patients referred for laboratory tests who are under age 45 is   14._____

   A. 7   B. 8   C. 9   D. 10

15. The OLDEST patient referred to the clinic during January was   15._____

   A. Jacqueline Adams   B. Linda James
   C. Arthur Lane   D. Jan Wilson

16. The ONLY patient treated in the Orthopedics clinic was   16._____

   A. Marie Cook   B. Pat Fisher
   C. Ellen Rogers   D. Jan Wilson

17. A woman, age 37, was referred from the Hematology clinic to the laboratory. Her labora-   17._____
    tory tests were performed on January 9. Her identification number would be

   A. 610937   B. 623709   C. 613790   D. 623790

18. A man was referred for lab tests from the Orthopedics clinic. He is 30 years old and his   18._____
    tests were performed on January 6. His identification number would be

   A. 413006   B. 510360   C. 513006   D. 513060

19. A 4 year old boy was referred from Pediatrics clinic to have laboratory tests on January   19._____
    23. His identification number was

   A. 310422   B. 310423   C. 310433   D. 320403

KEY (CORRECT ANSWERS)

1.	B		11.	D
2.	B		12.	B
3.	B		13.	A
4.	D		14.	C
5.	D		15.	D
6.	B		16.	A
7.	A		17.	B
8.	D		18.	C
9.	C		19.	B
10.	B			

———

TEST 4

DIRECTIONS: Questions 1 through 10 are to be answered on the basis of the information and directions given on the following page.

Assume that you are a Senior Stenographer assigned to the personnel bureau of a city agency. Your supervisor has asked you to classify the employees in your agency into the following five groups:

A. employees who are college graduates, who are at least 35 years of age but less than 50, and who have been employed by the. city for five years or more;

B. employees who have been employed by the City for less than five years, who are not college graduates, and who earn at least $32,500 a year but less than $34,500;

C. employees who have been city employees for five years or more, who are at least 21 years of age but less than 35, and who are not college graduates;

D. employees who earn at least $34,500 a year but less than $36,000 who are college graduates, and who have been employed by the city for less than five years;

E. employees who are not included in any of the foregoing groups.

NOTE: In classifying these employees you are to compute age and period of service as of January 1, 2003. In all cases, it is to be assumed that each employee has been employed continuously in City service. In each question, consider only the information which will assist you in classifying each employee. Any information which is of no assistance in classifying an employee should not be considered.

SAMPLE: Mr. Brown, a 29-year-old veteran, was appointed to his present position of Clerk on June 1, 2000. He has completed two years of college. His present salary is $33,050.

The correct answer to this sample is B, since the employee has been employed by the city for less than five years, is not a college graduate, and earns at least $32,500 a year but less than $34,500 .

DIRECTIONS: Questions 1 to 10 contain excerpts from the personnel records of 10 employees in the agency. In the correspondingly numbered space on the right print the capital letter preceding the appropriate group into which you would place each employee,

1. Mr. James has been employed by the city since 1993, when he was graduated from a local college. Now 35 years of age, he earns $36,000 a year.

1.____

2. Mr. Worth began working in city service early in 1999. He was awarded his college degree in 1994, at the age of 21.
As a result of a recent promotion, he now earns $34,500 a year.

2.____

3. Miss Thomas has been a City employee since August 1, 1998. Her salary is $34,500 a year. Miss Thomas, who is 25 years old, has had only three years of high school training.

3.____

4. Mr. Williams has had three promotions since entering city service on January 1, 1991. He was graduated from college with honors in 1974, when he was 20 years of age. His present salary is $37,000 a year.

4.____

5. Miss Jones left college after two years of study to take an appointment to a position in the city service paying $33,300 a year. She began work on March 1, 1997 when she was 19 years of age.

5.____

6. Mr. Smith was graduated from an engineering college with honors in January 1998 and became a city employee three months later. His present yearly salary is $35,810 . Mr. Smith was born in 1976.

6.____

7. Miss Earnest was born on May 31, 1979. Her education consisted of four years of high school and one year of business school. She was appointed as a typist in a city agency on June 1, 1997. Her annual salary is $33,500.

7.____

8. Mr. Adams, a 24-year-old clerk, began his city service on July 1, 1999, soon after being discharged from the U.S.
Army. A college graduate, his present annual salary is $33,200

8.____

9. Miss Charles attends college in the evenings, hoping to obtain her degree in 2004, when she will be 30 years of age. She has been a city employee since April 1998,and earns $33,350.

9.____

10. Mr. Dolan was just promoted to his present position after six years of city service. He was graduated from high school in 1982, when he was 18 years of age, but did not go on to college, Mr. Dolan's present salary is $33,500.

10.____

KEY (CORRECT ANSWERS)

1. A
2. D
3. E
4. A
5. C

6. D
7. C
8. E
9. B
10. E

TEST 5

DIRECTIONS: Questions 1 through 4 each contain five numbers that should be arranged in numerical order. The number with the lowest numerical value should be first and the number with the highest numerical value should be last. Pick that option which indicates the *correct* order of the numbers.

Examples:
A. 9; 18; 14; 15; 27
B. 9; 14; 15; 18; 27
C. 14; 15; 18; 27;   9
D. 9; 14; 15; 27; 18

The correct answer is B, which indicates the proper arrangement of the five numbers.

1. A. 20573; 20753; 20738; 20837; 20098
    B. 20098; 20753; 20573; 20738; 20837
    C. 20098; 20573; 20753; 20837; 20738
    D. 20098; 20573; 20738; 20753; 20837   1.____

2. A. 113492; 113429; 111314; 113114; 131413
    B. 111314; 113114; 113429; 113492; 131413
    C. 111314; 113429; 113492; 113114; 131413
    D. 111314; 113114; 131413; 113429; 113492   2.____

3. A. 1029763; 1030421; 1035681; 1036928; 1067391
    B. 1030421; 1029763; 1035681; 1067391; 1036928
    C. 1030421; 1035681; 1036928; 1067391; 1029763
    D. 1029763; 1039421; 1035681; 1067391; 1036928   3.____

4. A. 1112315; 1112326; 1112337; 1112349; 1112306
    B. 1112306; 1112315; 1112337; 1112326; 1112349
    C. 1112306; 1112315; 1112326; 1112337; 1112349
    D. 1112306; 1112326; 1112315; 1112337; 1112349   4.____

KEY (CORRECT ANSWERS)

1. D
2. B
3. A
4. C

TEST 6

DIRECTIONS: The phonetic filing system is a method of filing names in which the alphabet is reduced to key code letters. The six key letters and their equivalents are as follows:

KEY LETTERS	EQUIVALENTS
b	p, f, v
c	s, k, g, j , q, x, z
d	t
l	none
m	n
r	none

A key letter represents itself.
Vowels (a, e, i, o and u) and the letters w, h, and y are omitted.
For example, the name GILMAN would be represented as follows:

G is represented by the key letter C.
I is a vowel and is omitted.
L is a key letter and represents itself.
M is a key letter and represents itself.
A is a vowel and is omitted.
N is represented by the key letter M.

Therefore, the phonetic filing code for the name GILMAN is CLMM.
Answer questions 1 through 10 based on the information on the previous page.

1. The phonetic filing code for the name FITZGERALD would be   1._____

   A. BDCCRLD   B. BDCRLD   C. BDZCRLD   D. BTZCRLD

2. The phonetic filing code CLBR may represent any one of the following names EXCEPT   2._____

   A. Calprey   B. Flower   C. Glover   D. Silver

3. The phonetic filing code LDM may represent any one of the following names EXCEPT   3._____

   A. Halden   B. Hilton   C. Walton   D. Wilson

4. The phonetic filing code for the name RODRIGUEZ would be   4._____

   A. RDRC   B. RDRCC   C. RDRCZ   D. RTRCC

5. The phonetic filing code for the name MAXWELL would be   5._____

   A. MCLL   B. MCWL   C. MCWLL   D. MXLL

6. The phonetic filing code for the name ANDERSON would be   6._____

   A. AMDRCM   B. ENDRSM   C. MDRCM   D. NDERCN

7. The phonetic filing code for the name SAVITSKY would be   7._____

   A. CBDCC   B. CBDCY   C. SBDCC   D. SVDCC

8. The phonetic filing code CMC may represent any one of the following names EXCEPT   8._____

    A. James   B. Jayes   C. Johns   D. Jones

9. The *ONLY* one of the following names that could be represented by the phonetic filing   9._____
code CDDDM would be

    A. Catalano   B. Chesterton   C. Cittadino   D. Cuttlerman

10. The *ONLY* one of the following names that could be represented by the phonetic filing   10._____
code LLMCM would be

    A. Ellington   B. Hallerman   C. Inslerman   D. Willingham

---

KEY (CORRECT ANSWERS)

1. A
2. B
3. D
4. B
5. A

6. C
7. A
8. B
9. C
10. D

GLOSSARY OF TERMS
IN
MENTAL HEALTH, ALCOHOL ABUSE, DRUG ABUSE, AND MENTAL RETARDATION

CONTENTS

Page

GLOSSARY OF TERMS
IN
MENTAL HEALTH, ALCOHOL ABUSE, DRUG ABUSE, AND MENTAL RETARDATION

A LA CARTE RATE: A rate based on a specific itemization of services received by arecipient (even though the cost value of such services may be based on the average).

ACCOUNTANT (fiscal officer): A person who works with or is in charge of accountingactivities.

ACCOUNTING: The systematic recording and summarizing of business and financial transactions and analyzing, verifying and reporting results. Includes patient accounts.

ACTIVE RECIPIENT: A recipient currently under, the status of receiving direct services in the first through fourth order of interaction.

ADJUSTMENTS TO REVENUE: Both positive and negative adjustments to revenues such as donated service discounts, contractual adjustments, administrative adjustments and allowance for bad debts.

ADULT ACTIVITY SERVICE: A service designed to involve patients and participants inpursuing hobbies, playing games, serving, cooking, etc. The distinction between this and vocational rehabilitation is that none of the skills acquired would qualify the patient for paid employment.

ADMINISTERING AGENCY: The individual, group or corporation appointed, elected or otherwise designated in which ultimate responsibility and authority are vested for the conduct of the program, organization or organizational unit.

ADMINISTRATIVE ASSISTANT: A person who assists an administrator or is assigned certain routine administrative tasks which assist the administrator.

ADMINISTRATIVE OFFICER, CHIEF: A person appointed by the administering authority who has responsibility for directing a program and managing the resources for it.

ADMINISTRATIVE RESEARCH: Systematic observations or studies of the operations of organizations or their parts in relation to specific categories of interest (models of decision-making, flow of information, human stress and organizational change).

ADMINISTRATIVE STAFF: Staff members who provide the intraorganizational services (functions or support services) to clinical staff and to the organization itself,

AFFILIATION: Working relationships between organizations which are developed through contracts or agreements (usually written) for exchange or provision of services, training of staff, scientific advancement, professional counsel or administrative support.

ALCOHOL OR DRUG ADDICTION COUNSELOR: An individual often having had personal experiences in alcohol or drug addiction who works in a variety of counseling capacities with alcohol or drug abuse programs.

AUTHORITY: The explicit official or legal power or sanction which furnishes the grounds or justifies the provider organization's program.

BASIC RESEARCH: Systematic observations or experiments regarding throught, emotion or behavior in general or in relation to specific categories of disability (i.e., schizophrenia, mental retardation).

BASIC PROFESSIONAL EDUCATION: Experiences provided as practicum, field experiences, internships, residency training, etc. as part of the basic formal education leading to a degree.

BEHAVIOR MODIFICATION: The modification of individual behavior through systematic application of learning theory and principles. Includes application of operant conditioning techniques--the Skinner-Lindsley principles of systematically strengthening certain responses and weakening others--and of behavior shaping through differential reinforcement.

BLOCK: A well-defined piece of land bounded by streets or roads, railroad tracks,streams, other features on a map, or by invisible political boundaries.

BLOCK GROUP: Combination of blocks, approximately equal in area, which do not cut across census tract lines.

BLOCKFACE: A boundary segment of a block. A city block has a blockface on each side, usually with a range of house or building numbers.

BOARD CERTIFIED PSYCHIATRIST: A fully trained psychiatrist who is certified by the American Board of Psychiatry and Neurology, Inc.

BOARD ELIGIBLE PSYCHIATRIST: A psychiatrist who is fully trained and experienced, but has not yet been certified by American Board of Psychiatry and Neurology, Inc.

BUDGETING: Planning and allocation of fiscal resources to own organizational units, services and activities.

BUILDING AND LAND: The land, off-site capital utility improvements, roads, sidewalks , on-site, capital improvement, and buildings which are available for use by the organisation for its activities, functions and program.

BUILDING EXPENSES: Building rental, repairs, depreciation, light, heat, water and related building and land operating expenses.

BUSINESS OFFICER: A person who directs the supportive and fiscal services for a mental health program. This includes budget preparation and paying and accounting, purchasing, supply and inventory control, etc. It often also includes supervising food preparation, housekeeping and maintenance operations.

CARE SERVICES: Services related to providing for generic human needs for shelter, food, income, transportation and supervision.

CASE REVIEW: Staff conferences and case discussions of review to determine the assignment or reassignment of cases and appropriateness of treatment. Includes formal utilization review.

CASE-ORIENTED CONSULTATION: Consultation, the purpose of which is to assist the con-sultee in providing services to a specific client (individual, family group or therapy group) of the consultee.

CATCHMENT AREA: Geographical division from which recipients are admitted to a specified mental health organization for services. This usually refers to an area served by an organization.

CENSUS TRACT: Small permanent areas into which large cities and adjacent areas have been divided for the purpose of showing comparable small-area statistics. Census tract boundaries are determined by a local committee and approved by the Census Bureau. Census tracts conform to county lines and are designed to be relatively homogeneous in population characteristics, economic status and living conditions. The average tract has about 4,000 inhabitants.

CHAPLAIN OR PASTORAL COUNSELOR: A clergyman with special training in counseling parsons with emotional problems.

CHARACTERISTICS OF RECIPIENTS OF INDIVIDUAL-ORIENTED SERVICES: The descriptive qualifiers which further classify the recipient or, which singly or in combination, will uniquely identify or describe him, or which show his relation to the organization at a specific time.

CHEMOTHERAPY: Treatment by the use of medications. Includes tranquilizers, anti-depressants, anticonvulsants, sedatives, etc.

CLINICAL PROGRAM ADMINISTRATOR: A person who has responsibility for directing a clinical program or unit. (Medical director, clinical director, unit director)

CLINICAL OR COUNSELING PSYCHOLOGIST: A practitioner trained in psychological techniques including personality, aptitude, intelligence or memory testing, therapy, counseling, behavior modification and research.

CLINICAL RESEARCH: Systematic experiments to determine the causes, treatments and rehabilitation of various disabilities.

COLLATERAL TREATMENT OR COUNSELING: Treatment of the patient through interviews beyond the diagnostic level with collateral persons, such interviews centering around the patient's problems without the patient himself necessarily seen. Includes treatment of a child by working with the parents or the treatment of an oldster by working through family members.

COMMUNITY CARETAKERS: Individuals such as clergymen, lawyers, or family physicians who enroll in educational activities provided by a mental health program.

COMMUNITY-ORIENTED SERVICES: Services provided to representatives of other organizations, individual practitioners or to the general public, related to alcohol abuse, drug abuse, mental retardation, mental health in general or to related aspects of their recipients or programs.

COMMUNITY-ORIENTED SERVICE RECIPIENTS: Individuals or agents to whom community-oriented services are provided. (Synonym: indirect service recipient) The recipients above may further be classified according to whether they are facilities/ agencies, organization/ groups or private practitioners, and may be identified by additional words specifying exactly which agency, group or individual in the community is referred to.

COMMUNITY PLANNING AND DEVELOPMENT: Participation as a representative of an alcohol, drug abuse, mental retardation or mental health organization with community leaders, organizations and citizen groups, to plan for the enhancement and enrichment of the community and develop solutions for community problems.

CONSULTATION: A process of interaction between a staff of the organization (consultant) and representative(s) of another organization or individual practitioner (consultee) to assist the consultee, to impart behavioral science knowledge, skills or attitudes, and to aid the consultee in carrying out his mission(s).

CONTINUING EDUCATION: Short courses, workshops, etc., to update or enhance the clinical competencies of staff.

CONTRACTUAL ADJUSTMENT: An adjustment based on the uncollectable value of service rendered to a recipient which represents the difference between the full established rates for individual services and lower contractual rates.

CONTRACTUAL EXPENSES: Services purchased from another organization.

COST-FINDING: A system or method of allocating and reallocating costs from a point of data collection or original expenditure into different sets or subsets of costs, to charge all relevant costsdirect, indirect, or unassignedto other organizational units or final producing cost centers.

COUNSELING PSYCHOLOGIST: A psychologist whose special competence is in counseling clients, testing the interests of and giving professional guidance to individuals.

COUNTY: A primary political and administrative division of a state. In Louisiana these divisions are called parishes. In Alaska there are no counties and census statistics are shown for its election districts which are equivalent to counties.

COUNTY-CITY-LOCAL FUND REVENUE: Revenue received as authorized by any act of county, city or multi-level boards; legislative or executive branches of such governments other than fees in payment for specific services rendered.

COUPLE THERAPY: Treatment of intimate partners but excluding other significant family members, children or siblings. Includes married and "unmarried" couples.

DATA MANAGEMENT: Information collection, analysis and use of data and information designed to monitor and assess the functioning of the program, including routine statistical reporting or recipient characteristics, costs, efficiency, community characteristics, service loads and program efforts.

DEATH: (Specify level at time of death.) A change by the fact of a person's dying while in a recipient-status.

DEGREE OF IMPROVEMENT: A judgment of the degree of change in the recipient's condition. This is the traditional way of classifying recipient's results.

DEPARTMENT: Organizational unit whose purpose is to provide administrative and supportive services tp the organization itself.

DETOXIFICATION: Treatment by use of medication, rest, fluids and nursing care to restore physiological function after it has been upset by toxic agents such as alcohol or barbiturates.

DIDACTIC: Formal teaching in context of lectures, seminars, case conferences.

DIRECT COSTS: The costs that are charged directly to the organizational unit originally making the expenditure, regardless of their later reallocation (if any) to other organizational units or final producing cost centers.

DISCONTINUATION: (Specify level or combination of levels recipient is leaving). A "discontinuation" refers to the change of a person, other than by death, by removal from, leaving or discontinuing a recipient-status directly or through another person acting for him, in a specified level in a mental health system.

DIVISION: Organizational unit whose primary purpose is to recipients other than the organization itself.

DOMICILIARY SERVICES: A supervised residential program to provide an individual with total living care.

DONATED SERVICE DISCOUNT: An adjustment based on the uncollectable value of servicerendered to recipients who are financially unable to pay full established rates.

DONATIONS: "Revenue" which represents free contributions from individuals, corporations, charitable organizations, united community chests, foundations and others, other than above.

DOWN TIME: Activities which are not productive of individual-oriented, community-oriented, intraorganization-oriented, or manpower training and education services.

DUAL RATE: A rate which explicitly includes both 1) a fixed inclusive rate element unique to the type of service or program and 2) an a la carte rate element specific to the amount of time or specifically prescribed procedures or transactionr provided the recipient.

DUAL RESOURCE AFFILIATIONS: a) Contractee pays salaries or operating expenses of affiliate's organization for work or use at the affiliate's site; b) contractee's own staff, equipment, or materials are authorized for work or use at the affiliate's site.

EDUCATION AND VOCATIONAL EVALUATION: Evaluation to determine an individual's academic or vocational interests, aptitude, achievements.

ENUMERATION DISTRICT (ED): An area with small population (averaging 700) defined by the Census Bureau and used for the collection and tabulation of population and housing census data.

EQUIPMENT: The fixed, major movable or minor machinery, fixtures, articles, vehicles,apparatus, "things" and furniture which have a relatively long useful life and are not consumed in the course of a program.

EQUIPMENT EXPENSES: Equipment used, rental, repairs and depreciation expenses.

EVALUATIVE RESEARCH: Utilization of scientific research methods and techniques or the purpose of evaluating a program.

EXPENSES: The amount of resources, expressed in money, consumed in producing a service or carrying on an activity. (The service potential of the resources has been released and transformed into an expense.)

FACE-TO-FACE CONGREGATE COMMUNITY SESSION: Contact through continuous face-to-face group life or group living in a structured community setting.

FACE-TO-FACE GROUP INTERACTION CONTACT: Contact through face-to-face interaction, in person, with two or more people in which group interaction is one of the primary outcomes planned.

FACE-TO-FACE INDIVIDUAL CONTACT: Contact through face-to-face interaction with individuals and small groups (two, three or four people) where group interaction is not planned.

FACE-TO-FACE PRESENTATION TO GROUPS: Contact through lecture, speech or presentation to groups, where group interaction is not necessarily or primarily intended.

FACILITY: The plant, including buildings, grounds, supplies and equipment which are used or occupied by the organization or one of its units.

FACILITY MANAGEMENT: Day-to-day operations of the buildings, offices and grounds, including the maintenance, housekeeping, feeding, logistics, supply and related activities.

FAMILY TREATMENT OR COUNSELING: Treatment applied to the family as a unit. (All or significant members of the family are considered as recipients. This excludes groups of families and/or groups of married couples.)

FEDERAL FUND REVENUE: Revenue received as authorized by any act of Congress or the Executive Branch of the federal government, other than fees in payment for specific services rendered.

FEE: The net charge, expressed in money, which represents that portion of the set rate (9-E), plus or minus adjustments, if any, which ip billed to the recipient or third party payer.

FEE-FOR-SERVICE AFFILIATIONS: a) Affiliate directly bills the recipient or third party payer but receives no payments from the contractee; b) affiliate bills contractee, who in turn may or may not bill recipient or third party payer.

FEES FOR SERVICE: Revenue earned from charges made to recipients of services of the organization, including that portion paid by third party payers such as Medicare, Medicaid, compensation insurance, commercial insurance and other payers. This includes contract fees.

FIFTH ORDER INTERACTION: Intermittent delivery of services to a recipient on suspended, postponed or inactive status. Includes persons on waiting list, long term leave, provisional discharge or in a prepayment program status.

FIRST ADDITION: (Specify level or combination of levels coming into.) A "first addition" refers to the change of a person from Having had no prior recipient-status in a specified level in a mental health system to having current recipient status.

FIRST ORDER INTERACTION: Continuous delivery of services to a recipient pn a 24-hour basis in the service setting. Includes inpatient and resident care status.

FIXED COSTS: The costs which remain constant in total amount regardless of the level or fluctuation in the volume of program activity.

FIXED FEE AFFILIATIONS: a) Affiliate bills contractee at a fixed fee per calendar period regardless of services provided to recipient; b) affiliate-bills contractee at a fixed rate or per cent per calendar period, based on a variable such as staff hours expended, per cent bed occupancy, or other indirect indicator; c) contractee pays affiliate a lump-sum one-time payment for the performance of services.

FOURTH ORDER INTERACTION: Intermittent or brief services to a recipient on an unscheduled or casual contact basis. Includes walk-in contacts, unscheduled consultations and telephone calls status.

FULL RATE: The full established cost value, expressed in dollars, of the services rendered to recipients.

FUND RAISING: Promoting or lobbying for allocation of funds for own programs.

FUND REVENUE, OTHER: Revenue, other than donations, received from any other source than fees, federal, state, or local government sources, including gains on sale of assets, interest earned and miscellaneous other income, other than fees in payment for specific services rendered.

GENERAL (and special): "General" refers to facilities that provide treatment and care to persons who have a variety of medical conditions (e.g., a general hospital); "special" refers to facilities that provide treatment and care to persons who have specified medical conditions (e.g., a psychiatric hospital).

GENERALIZABLE RESEARCH: The study activities performed by staff of the organization for the production of scientific knowledge through testing of theories where it is the intent to follow scientific principles so that finding may be generalized beyond the immediate data or situation, or where the findings may be so general as to be only remotely germane to the immediate situation.

GEOGRAPHIC AREA RESIDENTS: The inhabitants of the total or subdivisions of the country who can be specified as living within identifiable boundaries.

GOAL (objective): A reality-constrained, time-specific, problem-oriented statement which specifies the desired change or end-state which an organization seeks to bring about. (Example: To educate all Portage County residents arrested for driving while under the influence of alcohol)

GOAL ATTAINMENT: Goals are set for each individual or community. Goals may be set in various terms such as "resolution of problems," "full employment," "independent social living," "reduced incidence of truancy." The extent to which the goal has been attained is then rated.

GROUP TREATMENT OR COUNSELING: Treatment by the use of group dynamics or group interaction. Includes group psychotherapy, group psychoanalysis, group play therapy, psychodrama, groups of families and/or groups of married couples, but excludes family therapy and group orientation, group intake or group diagnostic procedures.

HEARING EVALUATION: An evaluation to determine the cause and extent of hearing disorders and need for corrective work.

INACTIVE RECIPIENT: Individual for whom the organization has a defined responsibility by virtue of;contract or charge (HMO, group-insurance, welfare, clients, etc.) but who is not currently active or receiving services.

INCLUSIVE RATE: A periodic uniform rate, with variation for major type of service or program, established without regard to the specific level of utilization and without specific itemization of services received by a recipient.

INCOME MAINTENANCE: A service designed to provide the recipient with sufficient money or in-kind income to maintain a reasonable standard of living.

INDIGENOUS WORKER: A person whose primary qualification is his personal experience in the culture of the persons he serves, who works in a variety of counseling and behavior changing techniques in mental health programs or as an advocate for the clients of such programs.

INDIRECT COSTS: The costs that are reallocated from the organizational unit originally making the expenditure to another organizational unit which controls or influences the cost.

INDIVIDUAL TREATMENT OR COUNSELING: Treatment by individual interview. Includes supportive psychotherapy, relationship therapy, uncovering or insight psychoanalysis, counseling, play therapy, hypnotherapy (with or without the use of drugs) and casework treatment.

INDIVIDUAL-ORIENTED SERVICES: Services provided directly to a specific client (individual, collateral, family group or therapy group) in relation to their own positive mental health or to their own alcohol abuse, drug abuse, mental retardation or mental disorder problem.

INDIVIDUAL-ORIENTED SERVICE RECIPIENTS: Individuals for whom help is sought, families, collateral persons, therapy groups.

INFORMATION: Services which provide information about availability of services. Such services include crisis and information centers, 24-hour emergency (non face-to-face services and similar activities.

INFORMATION, SCREENING, REFERRAL: Services related to the availability, linkage, recipient's eligibility or suitability for own or other's programs.

IN-SERVICE EDUCATION: A systematic preparation of staff for the basic work they will perform in the agency.

INTERACTION INTENSITY: Degree of involvement and continuity between the recipient and provider of service.

INTERSTATE AREA: Combination of areas from two or more states such as Mid-Atlantic, East South Central, etc.

INTRAORGANIZATION SUPPORT FUNCTIONS: The activities or functions performed by or for the organization in which the direct recipient is the organization itself, and directed toward the support, maintenance and development of the organization itself.

INTRASTATE PLANNING AREA: A region within a given state usually comprising one or more counties with the division such that natural boundaries such as rivers or mountain ranges tend to give a certain economic or geographic homogeneity.

LAW: A statute enacted by a legislative branch, including the body of common law developed from judicial branch decisions, which expresses the binding custom, practice, conduct or action of an authority.

LEGAL STATUS: The legal authority, if any, by which a recipient enters and is held in a service-receiving status; there is considerable variation from state to state by differing statues. (Synonym: type of commitment)

LICENSED PRACTICAL OR LICENSED VOCATIONAL NURSE: A licensed nurse who has one year of practical nursing training.

LONG-TERM FACILITY: A long-term facility is defined as one in which over 50 percent of all patients admitted stay more than 30 days. However, in facilities such as residential drug units, different time durations may constitute long-term.

MANPOWER TRAINING ORIENTED SERVICES: A structured educational process of imparting job-related knowledge, skills and attitudes to individual practitioners and members of your own or of other organization (regular staff, volunteers, students or indigenous workers), to directly increase the recipient(s) knowledge, skills, attitudes or work effectiveness.

MANUAL, PHYSICAL AND RELATED TRANSACTIONS: Physical operation of equipment, machines, tools or appliances or physical handling of materials, supplies and other objects.

MEAL SERVICE: A service designed to provide the necessary food and nutritional requirements of the recipient in prepared meal.

MEDICAL SPECIALIST, OTHER: A physician who is specially trained or certified in one of the various specialtiesradiologist, internist, pathologist, etc.

MEDICAL-SURGICAL SERVICE, OTHER: Other medical, dental or surgical procedures directed to general physical health.

MENTAL HEALTH AIDE OR ASSISTANT: A New Careers level mental health worker with only in-service education or technical school education who works in a community mental health program under the supervision of professionals.

MENTAL HEALTH MANPOWER TRAINING RECIPIENTS: Individuals, groups or organizations who receive the educational and training services of a program.

MENTAL HEALTH NURSE: A registered nurse who specializes in working with communities about the public health aspects of persons with emotional problems or about the prevention of such problems.

MENTAL HEALTH TECHNICIAN (mental health associate): A person with 1 or 2 years of formal training (perhaps an associate degree) who carries out a range of individual and community-oriented services in mental health programs.

MENTAL HEALTH WORKER: A paraprofessional worker with an associate degree or other training or experience in mental health who performs a variety of techniques on behalf of patients and their families either in institutions or in communities. These persons work in an organized system under the general supervision of other mental health professionals.

MILIEU THERAPY: Treatment by a structured total physical, psychological and social environment to meet the needs of the individual or group of recipients.

MISSION: A general group of program objectives which have one or more characteristics in common. (Example: alcohol preventive mission)

MONEY: Cash, investments, receivables, and budgeted-to-be-received operating funds which are available for use by the organization for its activities, functions andprogram.

MOVEMENT CHANGES OF RECIPIENT OF INDIVIDUAL-ORIENTED SERVICE: The progress of an individual in or out of a system, from one recipient category to another, or from one program, organizational unit, site or interaction intensity status to another.

MUTUAL INTEREST AFFILIATIONS: a) Contractee and affiliate, in consortium, receive operating or capital construction monies from a common funding agency based on agreement to cooperate in their mutual use; b) contractee and affiliate share salaries and other operating or capital expenses to perform work of benefit to each or to mutual recipients; c) eachthe contractee and affiliatebears own expenses with no exchange of monies, but agree to the free flow of recipients between them, the sharing of records and information, and the continuance of staff responsibility for recipients regardless of location.

NEUROLOGICAL EVALUATION: A complete examination of the central, peripheral and sympathetic nervous system, noting observations and findings supplemented by diagnosis, if indicated.

NEUROLOGIST: A physician who is specially trained in the diagnosis and treatment of diseases of the nervous system.

NEWSPAPERS, MAGAZINES: Contact through mass media messages in newspapers, magazines,journals, newsletters and other regular or special news publications.

NON-WORK ACTIVITIES: Activities that do not directly relate to the staff's^ responsibilities or the organization's programs, objectives or goals.

NURSE: A practitioner of nursing who is registered or licensed in nursing by state law.

NURSE, REGISTERED: A nurse who is registered to practice nursing by a state board of nurse registration.

OBJECTIVE (goal): A concise description of a desired end state sought at a specified future point in time, related to a human need. (Example: reduce alcohol-related motor vehicle deaths 20% by 1975.)

OCCUPATIONAL THERAPIST:, A practitioner trained in occupational therapy who uses arts and crafts techniques in the treatment and rehabilitation of patients.

OFF DUTY OR DOWN TIME ACTIVITIES: Sick leave, vacation, compensatory time off, mealor break time activities, waiting and other personal non-work activities.

ON CALL: Prearranged waiting, holding oneself available for potential demands or requests for services.

ON LEAVE: Time spent away from work while on vacation, sick leave, compensatory time, administrative leave, military leave, jury duty and miscellaneous absences or tardinesses.

OPERATING EXPENSES, OTHER: Printing, publications, subscriptions, dues, fees, licenses and other related expenses.

OPERATING SUPPLIES: Supplies, articles and materials used and related expenses.

ORGANIZATION: An administrative and functional structure and a grouping of persons within that structural entity defined by law, charter, license, contract and agreement to carry out enunciated purposes or missions.

ORGANIZATIONAL UNIT: A component of the organization established for the delivery of services to which specific resources are assigned.

ORGANIZING: Establishing conceptual relationships among component staff and units of the organization, services and resources, as a necessary precedent to action.

ORIENTATION PROGRAMS: Orientation to the objectives and procedures of the agency.

OUTPUT UNITS: Amounts of services provided expressed in terms of adopted units of services reflecting the costs of resources expended.

PERSON HOURS: Hours and minutes of staff time expended.

PERSONAL: Activities related to coffee, lunch and rest breaks.

PERSONAL ADJUSTMENT TRAINING: Provision of training in self-help and motor skills, habit training, self-care training, toilet training, activities of daily living and social development preliminary to special education or other placement.

PERSONAL CARE: A service designed to assist a recipient perform the routine tasks of daily living such as bathing, hair care, mouth care, feeding, personal hygiene, toileting, shaving, dressing, grooming and escorting on foot.

PERSONNEL: The clinical and administrative staff employees, volunteers, consultants and residents/students-in-placement who are available to perform the activities and functions of a program.

PERSONNEL EXPENSES: Salaries and wages, employee benefits and consultant fee expenses.

PERSONNEL OFFICER: A person who recruits staff, prepares payrolls, maintains personnel records, manages grievance procedures and performs related personnel functions.

HYSICAL EVALUATION: A complete examination of the body noting observations and findings, supplemented by diagnosis, if indicated.

PHYSICIAN: An individual who is licensed to practice medicine.

PHYSICIAN, GENERAL: A physician who is licensed to practice general medicine.

PLANNING AND EVALUATION OFFICER: A person who estimates, projects and identifies trends and needs of the program and the community, initiates plans for program changes to meet.these needs and evaluates the degree of success in meeting needs.

POLICY: A statement of philosophy and direction which guides the conduct of the organization.

POTENTIAL RECIPIENT AT LARGE: Individual who has no relationship to the organization unless or until a situation arises for which services are required. (i.e., catchment area target population)

POTENTIAL RECIPIENT CONTACT: A recipient under the status of receiving information/ screening/referral services. (Synonym: information-referral-screening recipient, inquirer, pre-patient.

PRACTICUM: Supervision and informal teaching of trainees in the course of their assigned experience with recipients (including rounds, team meetings).

PREPARATION FOR TRAINING: Course design, preparation for presentations, reading.

PRESENTING PROBLEM: This is typically presented from the viewpoint of the client rather than from in-depth psychopathological interpretation of staff: work, social relations, physical complaints, sexuality, suicide, anxiety/depression, alcohol drug abuse, psychopathologic symptoms, etc.

PROBLEM EVALUATION, EXAMINATION, ASSESSMENT: Services related to identifying the detailed nature and extent of the recipient's condition and formulating a plan for services.

PROBLEM EVALUATIONS, OTHER: Many other problem evaluations not unique to mental health are also provided (e.g., laboratory, dental, electroencephalogram, etc.).

PROBLEM RESOLUTION: The presenting problem of individuals or the community are categorized and rated as to whether the problems have been mitigated. (Example: less frequent bed wetting, decreased suicidal rate)

PROCEDURE: A particular series of operational steps to be followed in order to implement a policy.

PROGRAM: A set of related organizations, resources, and/or program transactions directed to the accomplishment of a defined jset of objectives for a specified target population or a specified geographic area.

PROGRAM AND ORGANIZATION DEVELOPMENT: Sessions for developing and implementing new program directions for the agency.

PROGRAM APPROPRIATENESS: The extent to which programs are directed toward those problems that are believed to have the greatest importance, based on the philosophy and the value systems of decision-makers.

PROGRAM CLINICAL STAFF AND TECHNOLOGISTS: Staff members who are licensed or otherwise qualified to provide individual-oriented, community-oriented, manpower development or research services of the program.

PROGRAM EFFICIENCY: The cost in resources of attaining objectives; the relationship between effort and effect, or input and output; evaluation in terms of cost (money, time, personnel, public convenience); a ratio between effort and achievement, the capacity of an individual, organization, facility, operation or activity to produce results in proportion to the effort expended.

PROGRAM EFFECTIVENESS: The extent to which pre-established program objectives are attained as a result of program activity; the results of effort relative to an immediate goal; the degree or extent to which success is achieved in resolving a' problem.

PROGRAM EFFORT: The quantity and quality of activity that takes place or of resources that are consumed.

PROGRAM EVALUATION: Determining the degree to which a program is meeting its objectives, the problems it is encountering and the side effects it is creating.

PROGRAM OUTCOME: The effects achieved for a target population by a program.

PROGRAM PLANNING: The process of designing and adjusting the organization's program activities and services to its program purposes, objectives, goals and priorities.

PROGRAM PURPOSE: A general statement of intent about a range of human needs or problems of a target population to which an organization addresses its services.

PROGRAM SIDE EFFECTS: All effects of program operation other than attainment of objectives. These side effects may be desirable or undesirable and may be anticipated or unanticipated.

PROGRAM-ORIENTED CONSULTATION: Consultation, the purpose of which is to assist the consultee in planning and developing his program or in solving his own program system problems.

PSYCHIATRIC AIDE, PSYCHIATRIC TECHNICIAN OR ATTENDANT: A worker who provides ward level psychiatric care and treatment to mental patients often under supervision of a nurse after a period of inservice training.

PSYCHIATRIC EVALUATION: The psychodiagnostic process, including a medical history and mental status, which notes the attitudes, behavior, estimate of intellectual functioning, memory functioning, orientation and an inventory of the patient's assets in a descriptive (but not an interpretative) fashion; impressions and recommendations.

PSYCHIATRIC NURSE: A registered nurse who specializes in working with psychiatric patients.

PSYCHIATRIC RESIDENT: A physician still in specialty training to become a psychiatrist.

PSYCHIATRIC SOCIAL WORKER: A social worker who specializes in work with mental patients and their families.

PSYCHIATRIST: A physician who is trained in the diagnosis and treatment of mentaldisorders.

PSYCHOANALYST: A psychiatrist who has special training in and uses the technique of psychoanalysis with his clients.

PSYCHOLOGICAL EVALUATION AND TESTING: The evaluation of cognitive processes and emotions and problems of adjustment in individuals or in groups, through interpretation of tests of mental abilities, aptitudes, interests, attitudes, emotions, motivation and personality characteristics, including the interpretation of psychological tests of individuals.

PSYCHOLOGICAL TECHNICIAN: A person trained in psychology who performs limited psychological functions under rather close supervision.

PSYCHOMETRIST: A psychologist who specializes in tests of measurement such as intelligence tests.

PSYCHOSOCIAL EVALUATION: The determination and examination of the social situation of the individual related to family background, family interaction, living arrangements, psycho-/or socioeconomic problems, treatment evaluation and statement of future goals and plans.

PUBLIC INFORMATION AND PUBLIC EDUCATION: A one-way educational process of imparting knowledge to and changing attitudes of the general public, segments of the population or special target groups to increase understanding of positive mental health and mental disorder and availability of resources.

PUBLIC INFORMATION OFFICER: A person who prepares and disseminates information regarding the program for the public media, the general public and for special publics. He may also have public relations responsibilities for assuring an accurate image of the program.

PUBLIC RELATIONS: Activities for developing reciprocal understanding and goodwill between the organization and the public, other organizations, and other alcohol, drug abuse, mental retardation and mental health programs.

PURCHASING AGENT: A person who purchases supplies and equipment.

READDITION: (Specify level or combination of levels coming into.) A "readdition" refers to the change of a person (who has had prior recipient-status on a specified level in a mental health system) from no immediate prior recipient-status to having current recipient-status.

RECIPIENT: A person, family, collateral person, group, organization or general public who receives or is eligible for the services of a specified organization by virtue of membership in the largest population.

RECIPIENT DAYS (patient days): Days (or fractions) of recipient (patient) time expended.

RECIPIENT OF MANPOWER TRAINING: Students from institutions of higher education, staff of own agency, community caretakers, other agency's staff.

RECIPIENT REIMBURSEMENT STATUS: The source from which an organization is reimbursed for services provided to a recipient. (Synonym: pay status)

RECIPIENT SATISFACTION: Reports by individuals or community recipients regarding their degree of satisfaction or improvement.

RECORD-KEEPING, OTHER: Preparation, updating, filing, retrieval, and use of records related to office communications, work flow, scheduling and facility operations.

RECORDS MANAGEMENT: Patient-client clinical records: Preparation and updating of health and other records necessary for the provision of individual-oriented services, including scoring and report writing related to psychological tests. Includes notating in clinical records by staff.

RECORDS OFFICER, CLINICAL: A person responsible for the organization and maintenance of clinical records of recipients. (Medical record administrator in hospital unit)

RECREATION THERAPIST: A practitioner who uses recreational skills and techniques in the treatment and rehabilitation of patients.

REFERRAL: Services which direct, guide or link the recipient to other appropriate community resources.

REFERRAL SOURCE: The individual, agency or group who recommended service to recipient or recipient to service.

REGULATION: A rule or order having the force of law issued by an executive branch of government to control custom, practice or conduct.

REHABILITATION, RESTORATION, HABILITATION SERVICES: Services related to preparing or training a person to function within the limits of the original or residual disability by the acquisition, return or accommodation to loss of skills, knowledge.

RESEARCH OR PROGRAM ANALYST: A person who plans, organizes, performs studies and prepares reports about the program's effectiveness and efficiency or does independent research studies.

RESOURCES: The personnel, equipment, supplies, physical structures and money, owned or controlled, which are the source of supply or support of the operation of an organization.

REVENUES: The amount of all potential income, at the program's full established rates, of all services rendered to recipients, regardless of the amounts actually paid by or on behalf of the recipient, including both fee and fund revenues.

ROOM AND SHELTER: A service designed to provide the necessary sleeping and living space to the recipient.

RURAL PLACE: That portion of some area which is not classified as urban.

SCREENING: Activities which determine the type and extent of the problem of the individual seeking help, conducted by persons competent to make such judgements.

SECOND ORDER INTERACTION: Continuous delivery of services to a recipient for a substantial portion of a 24-hour period in the service setting. Includes day, night, weekend, half-way, quarter-way, millieu and therapeutic communities, classes and conferences, etc...status and may be subclassified accordingly.

SERVICE MISSION: One or more related activities or transactions between the recipient and provider, or on behalf of the recipient or a third party, which is intended to produce a defined outcome.

SESSION: Face-to-face staff-to-group. (See Part 6-B.)

SET RATE: The established charge which to varying degrees reflects the cost value of the services provided to recipients.

SHELTERED WORK: A service in which the handicapped may receive 1) work evaluation; 2) social and personal adjustment training; 3) vocational skill training; 4) extended employment either in transition to outside employment or as a terminal work adjustment (may be reported separately).

SHORT-TERM FACILITIES: A short-term facility is one in which over 50 per cent of all patients admitted stay less than 30 days. However, in facilities such as residential drug units, different time durations may constitute short-term.

SITE: The local place or scene at which the provider staff are present at the time services are delivered.

SIXTH ORDER INTERACTION: Receiving no services of any kind but has the status of being a member of the target population.

SOCIAL REHABILITATION SERVICE: The process of helping an individual in his psycho-social adjustment by learning or relearning social skills. Includes occupational therapy, industrial therapy, recreational therapy, resocialization programs and music therapy.

SOCIAL WORK CASE AIDE OR TECHNICIAN: A practitioner who works under the supervision of a social worker to carry limited social work responsibilities.

SOCIAL WORKER: A practitioner specially trained in social and community techniques to help families and patients with their social problems and adjustment to community.

SOCIAL WORKER, GENERIC: A practitioner with an MSW or Bachelor's degree in social work, but not specialized.

SOCIO-EPIDEMIOLOGICAL RESEARCH: Studies to determine incidence and prevalence of various disabilities and problems related to socioeconomic and epidemiclogical factors.

SOMATIC TREATMENT: Treatment of mental disorder by the use of physical procedures other than chemotherapy or detoxification. Includes electroconvulsive therapy, insulin therapy, narcotherapy, hydrotherapy, etc.

SPECIAL EDUCATION AND TUTORING SERVICE: Training and teaching of the mentally retarded and emotionally disturbed to increase their social, academic and vocational skills.

REHABILITATION, RESTORATION, HABILITATION SERVICES: Services related to preparing or training a person to function within the limits of the original or residual disability by the acquisition, return or accommodation to loss of skills, knowledge.

RESEARCH OR PROGRAM ANALYST: A person who plans, organizes, performs studies and prepares reports about the program's effectiveness and efficiency or does independent research studies.

RESOURCES: The personnel, equipment, supplies, physical structures and money, owned or controlled, which are the source of supply or support of the operation of an organization.

REVENUES: The, .amount ,of all., potential income, at the program's full established rates, of all services rendered to recipients, regardless of the amounts actually paid by or on behalf of the recipient, including both fee and fund revenues.

ROOM AND SHELTER: A service designed to provide the necessary sleeping and living space to the recipient.

RURAL PLACE: That portion of some area which is not classified as urban.

SCREENING: Activities which determine the type and extent of the problem of the individual seeking help, conducted by persons competent to make such judgements.

SECOND ORDER INTERACTION: Continuous delivery of services to a recipient for a substantial portion of a 24-hour period in the service setting. Includes day, night, weekend, half-way, quarter-way, millieu and therapeutic communities, classes and conferences, etc...status and may be subclassified accordingly.

SERVICE MISSION: One or more related activities or transactions between the recipient and provider, or on behalf of the recipient or a third party, which is intended to produce a defined outcome.

SESSION: Face-to-face staff-to-group. (See Part 6-B.)

SET RATE: The established charge which to varying degrees reflects the cost value of the services provided to recipients.

SHELTERED WORK: A service in which the handicapped may receive 1) work evaluation; 2) social and personal adjustment training; 3) vocational skill training; 4) extended employment either in transition to outside employment or as a terminal work adjustment (may be reported separately).

SHORT-TERM FACILITIES: A short-term facility is one in which over 50 per cent of all patients admitted stay less than 30 days. However, in facilities such as residential drug units, different time durations may constitute short-term.

SITE: The local place or scene at which the provider staff are present at the time services are delivered.

SIXTH ORDER INTERACTION: Receiving no services of any kind but has the status of being a member of the target population.

SOCIAL REHABILITATION SERVICE: The process of helping an individual in his psycho-social adjustment by learning or relearning social skills. Includes occupational therapy, industrial therapy, recreational therapy, resocialization programs and music therapy.

SOCIAL WORK CASE AIDE OR TECHNICIAN: A practitioner who works under the supervision of a social worker to carry limited social work responsibilities.

SOCIAL WORKER: A practitioner specially trained in social and community techniques to help families and patients with their social problems and adjustment to community.

SOCIAL WORKER, GENERIC: A practitioner with an MSW or Bachelor's degree in social work, but not specialized.

SOCIO-EPIDEMIOLOGICAL RESEARCH: Studies to determine incidence and prevalence of various disabilities and problems related to socioeconomic and epidemiclogical factors.

SOMATIC TREATMENT: Treatment of mental disorder by the use of physical procedures other than chemotherapy or detoxification. Includes electroconvulsive therapy, insulin therapy, narcotherapy, hydrotherapy, etc.

SPECIAL EDUCATION AND TUTORING SERVICE: Training and teaching of the mentally retarded and emotionally disturbed to increase their social, academic and vocational skills.

SPECIAL TEACHER: A certified teacher with special preparation for working with the mentally retarded, emotionally disturbed or children with special learning disabilities.

SPECIAL THERAPISTS, OTHER: Practitioners who use specific skills and techniques in the treatment and rehabilitation of patients. (They may be classified by the technique such as art, music, drama, etc.)

SPEECH AND HEARING THERAPY: Corrective work for such disorders.

SPEECH EVALUATION: An evaluation to determine the cause and extent of speech disorders and need for corrective work.

STAFF: The personnel or combination of personnel who perform the activities and functions that comprise the services of a program.

STAFF ENHANCEMENT: Professional advancement or enrichment for the benefit of the recipients.

STAFF-ORIENTED CONSULTATION: Consultation, the purpose of which is to improve the knowledge, skills, attitudes or insights of the consultee himself, or to help him with crises associated with his emotional or related problems.

STAFFING-RECRUITING: The classifying, specifying, recruiting, selecting, placing and promoting of the organization's personnel.

STANDARD: A state or condition accepted as a minimal or exemplary condition, appearing in law, regulation or policy.

STANDARD METROPOLITAN STATISTICAL AREA (SMSA): Consists of a county or group of counties containing at least one city (or "twin cities") having 50,000 inhabitants or more (central city), plus adjacent counties that are metropolitan in character and are economically and socially integrated with the central city. The name of the central city is used as the name of the SMSA. In New England, SMSA's are defined in terms of cities and towns.

STATE: The major political units of the United States.

STATE FUND REVENUE: Revenue received as authorized by any act of state legislatures or executive branches of state governments other than fees in payment for specific services rendered.

STATISTICIAN: A person responsible for gathering, maintaining, analyzing, reporting and interpreting aggregate data about the recipients, staff and services of a program.

STEP-VARIABLE COSTS: The costs which vary over a wide range of program activity but do not fluctuate directly in proportion to some measure of program activity.

SUITABILITY DETERMINATION: Services intended to provide information about the availability or eligibility of a person for another organization's services.

SUPERVISED OBSERVATION: A service designed to provide the recipient with a protective, concerned observer, to gather information or to protect the recipient from harming himself, others or material goods.

SUPERVISING-DIRECTING: The assignment of tasks and review of performance to see that personnel perform appropriately.

SUPPLIES: The expendable articles and materials such as office, wearing apparel, Pharmaceuticals, housekeeping, dietary, fuel, audio-visual tapes, laboratory,testing, educational materials and supplies, etc.

SUPPLY OFFICER: A person who manages the inventories and stocks of supplies and equipment.

SUPPORT TRANSACTIONS, OTHER: Dictation, transcribing, case-recording, filing, typing, proof-reading, scheduling, billing, fee collection, drug dispensing, bookkeeping and related support transactions.

TARGET POPULATION: The population group or subgroup toward which the services of programs, organizations and organizational units are directed.

TEAM: Organizational units which consist of officially designated multi-disciplinary staff groups who coordinate and supplement their skills to provide services to recipients other than the organization itself, or the organization itself.

TEAM, EVALUATION: A team in which each specialist provides his specialty services as he feels they are indicated; evaluation decisions are made at team conferences.

TEAM, CLINICAL: A team of clinical staff and technologists officially designated who coordinate and supplement their skills to provide individual-oriented services to recipients other than the organization itself.

TEAM, CO-EQUAL: A team of workers in which there is no "captain," but each member is equal in making decisions. Roles of various team members may vary from day to day.

TEAM, MEDICAL (psychiatric) OR TREATMENT: A team of various professionals whose efforts are all directed by a physician or psychiatrist. This is the traditional treatment team.

TEAM, ONE-WORKER COORDINATED: A team in which the recipient has a single person, often a mental health worker, as his major coordinator for the decisions and activities of the team.

TEAM, REHABILITATION: A team of workers concerned primarily with the rehabilitation of the recipient and usually directed by a vocational counselor.

TECHNIQUES AND KNOWLEDGE: The sum of what is known and the technical methods for applying the body of knowledge, information and principles about mental illness, mental retardation, alcohol abuse, drug abuse and human behavior in general.

TELEPHONE INDIVIDUAL CONTACT: Contact by telephone with individuals and small groups to, from or about recipient.

TELEVISION, RADIO, MOTION PICTURE FILM OR AUDIO RECORDING: Contact through radio, television, film, or recording of lectures, panel discussion, interviews, demonstrations or documentary programs.

THERAPEUTIC COMMUNITY: Treatment by the use of continuous controlled congregate community living and manipulation of the community dynamics of the members of that community.

THIRD ORDER INTERACTION: Intermittent delivery of servcies to a recipient on a periodic scheduled short visit basis. Includes a scheduled outpatient service, regularly scheduled short training sessions and consultation status.

TRAINING OFFICER: A person who organizes and directs training functions such as orientation programs, in-service training, affiliate programs for professional students, continuing education and organizational development programs for staff.

TRANSACTION MODE: The generic method used by the provider staff in delivering services or performing support functions.

TRANSACTION UNITS: Simple count of the number of various services or steps carried out or completed.

TRANSPORTATION: A service designed to provide the recipient with the means to travel or to move about from place to place, by auto, bus or other conveyance.

TRAVEL: Physical movement from one location to another by auto, bus, rail or air transportation.

TREATMENT OR COUNSELING SERVICES: Services related to the reduction of disability or discomfort, amelioration of signs and symptoms and changes in specific physical, mental or social functioning.

UNITED STATES: Fifty states and the District of Columbia, excluding outlying areas of American Samoa, Canal Zone, Commonwealth of Puerto Rico.

UNRELATED MEETINGS, CONFERENCES, WORKSHOPS: Participation'in such meetings, conferences or workshops that do not directly relate to the mission, objectives or goals of the organization.

URBAN PLACE: The term "place" refers to a concentration of population, regardless of legally prescribed units, powers or function. Urban places include all incorporated and unincorporated places of 2,500 or more and the towns, townships and counties classified as urban.

VARIABLE COSTS: The costs that are expected to fluctuate directly in proportion to some measure of program activity (such as the number of patients in beds; such as the number of patient-interviews).

VISITS: Face-to-face staff-to-others, individual contacts to include interviews and visits for the purpose of observation or visual inspection.

VOCATIONAL COUNSELOR: A practitioner trained in vocational testing and counseling who uses these techniques in the vocational and social rehabilitation of patients.

VOCATIONAL REHABILITATION, COUNSELING: Process to assist an individual in developing work skills, habits and attitudes and to assist him in job placement.

VOLUNTEER: A person who offers his services in a program free of charge. Most often these are part-time workers.

VOLUNTEER, GROUP: A person who provides his services as a member of a group (i.e., women's club, a fraternity, a church group). These services are often of a social or recreational kind.

VOLUNTEER, INDIVIDUAL: A person who offers his services as an individual (i.e., an art instructor, a foster grandparent).

VOLUNTEERS, DIRECTOR OF: A person who recruits, orients, assigns and assures the appropriate use of a volunteer staff. WAITING: Unarranged waiting for an activity to begin.

WRITTEN MESSAGE, INDIVIDUAL: Contact by individual letter, memorandum, telegram or other written message to, from or about recipient.

WRITTEN, OTHER: Contact through special pamphlet, poster, brochure, leaflets, flyers, textbooks, instructional material, etc.

WRITTEN TEST, INDIVIDUAL: Contact through administration of a written or mixed oral and written test, examination or observation test.

ZIP CODE AREA OR ZIP AREA: A numbered area for directing and sorting mail. Zip areas are established by the U.S. Post Office and may change according to postal requirements.

———